GOOD
TO THE
LAST
DROP!

**Embracing Your
Life's Third Chapter**

Copyright © 2024 Irene Weinburg

ISBN: 979-8-9904011-0-5 - Paperback
ISBN: 979-8-9904011-1-2 - Hardcover

All rights reserved. This book or any portion thereof may not be reproduced or used in any manner whatsoever without the express written permission of the publisher except for the use of brief quotations in a book review.

Printed in the United States of America
First Printing, 2024

Editor: Mary Metcalfe

Dedicated to my three cherished grandsons –

David, Noah, and Aaron.

Thank you for infusing my Third Chapter with immense love and joy!

I love you always, Gaga!

CONTENTS

Foreword
vii

Part 1 - Grief and Rebirth
1

My Celebration of Life! - Irene Weinberg
3

The Letter - Casey Gauntt
7

Awakening Through Grief - Angela Clement
15

Witnessed - Shirley Lyster
21

Decades of Learning to Love my Life to Death - Yvonne Heath
27

Developing Compassion Through Trauma - Ellie Pechet
37

The Five Pillars of Healing Grief - Mark Ireland
45

Part 2 - Embracing Life, Reinvention, and New Purpose
53

My Journey from Audiologist to Perinatal Bereavement Specialist, and a Few Things in Between - Julie Lazar-Reskakis
55

Mother of Reinvention - Phyllis Okon
59

Cosmic Dreamer - Betty Jampel
65

Finding Meaning in Solitude and Community - Jeff Rasley
73

A Lifetime of Resilience, Renewal, and Reinvention - Alan Stein
81

From Personal Tragedy to Public Triumph:
The Creation of "Grief 2 Growth" - Brian Smith
89

Embracing Life's Tapestry With Animals - Tami Hendrix
95

Journey Beyond: Exploring the
Mysteries of Life, Death, and Creation - Julie Ryan
101

Part 3 - Living Your Best Life
105

A Mother's Love and The Promise - Faust Ruggiero
107

Grateful for the Journey - Frances Rae Key
113

Living My Best Life - Roz Weinberger
121

A Work in Progress - Mary Metcalfe
125

We're Never Too Old to be Part of the Solution - Robert (Bob) Wells
133

Becoming a Wise One Embracing and Celebrating Later
Stages of Your Earthly Experience - Mark Pitstick
139

My Path to Joy - Anita Albright
147

Spilling the Tea on Choice - Heidi Connolly
155

How I Met Myself - Mary D'Agostino
161

Contributors
169

Acknowledgments
179

Looking for Irene?
181

Suggestions for Online References
183

Selected Bibliography
185

Excerpt - They Serve Bagels in Heaven
189

GOOD TO THE LAST DROP!

Embracing Your Life's Third Chapter

Irene Weinberg

FOREWORD

*"Instead of saying 'how old are you?' people
should say 'how long have you lived?'"*

—Diane Von Furstenberg

Good to the Last Drop! is a book for all of us living our Third Chapter of life in these early years of the twenty-first century. Let's be honest: we're living in a period that will mark human history for generations to come. Just as two world wars, a global depression, and numerous armed conflicts and economic recessions have left their mark on earlier generations of the twentieth century, the twenty-first century will be remembered as a time of sea changes: in our environment, in politics and governance, in civil society, in cultures and economies around the world. The status quo is being challenged daily everywhere we look.

However, amid these many challenges facing our third planet from the sun, there is a role for each one of us to make a positive difference, no matter our age or abilities. As you'll read in these personal stories in *Good to the Last Drop!*, each writer has faced some of the most difficult challenges known to humanity: the tragic loss of a child or spouse years before their time, the challenges of poor health or disability personally or in family members. And for all, the life-affirming recognition that there is more to seeing this life than as simply a beginning, middle, and then end.

Good to the Last Drop! is for people who have faced or are now facing situations that have challenged their assumptions about life and death, their spirituality, the fairness of the universe, how we grieve, and whether it's possible to ever find joy and happiness again. The authors come from a variety of belief backgrounds, ranging from theism to agnosticism to atheism and all points in between.

Many researchers and authors have explored and discussed life from the perspective of three distinct chapters in life. While the Third Chapter has several meanings and definitions in academic literature and the media, the following generally encompass the three chapters:

Chapter 1:   Youth – formative years

Chapter 2:   Adulthood – work, family, community

Chapter 3:   Senior – retirement, legacy years

By the time we enter our Third Chapter in our fifties and sixties and beyond, we have explored and experienced life through many personal challenges: starting or ending relationships, raising families, pursuing our calling or careers, as well as learning about ourselves and our relationship to the world around us. However, many of us enter our Third Chapter without any real plan for how we will spend our remaining years. We hope for good health for as long as possible, we hope our financial situation will make retirement possible, we may plan to travel, write a book, take up a new hobby, or perhaps teach.

There are so many possibilities but, for many, there are also life-altering challenges: loss of independence, loss of mobility, the illness and death of a loved one, chronic illness or pain, change in financial situation. Just when you hope for the "golden years" to become a reality, the "rusting years" set in. For those who are caught unawares, and that may be most of us, the reality is that we find ourselves facing the unknown – sometimes with no warning or ability to prepare.

Intellectually, we understand that every person we know will someday pass on or 'transition', as people are increasingly describing the end of physical life. That doesn't make it easier when it happens. And if that time has been preceded by months or years of caregiving and watching a loved one fade away from physical or cognitive diseases, the grieving may well start while our loved one is still alive.

Some people in their Third Chapter think of it as the beginning of the end rather than a time to find renewed purpose and seek out new challenges – to leave a positive legacy. Yet others find a way to move forward despite challenges, to continue making a difference, and to contribute to personal, community, and social well-being.

In the years since I started my *Grief and Rebirth* podcast, I have interviewed many dozens of people who have found a way forward after times of great trauma, loss, grief, and ultimately 'rebirth'. Their journeys of healing, combined with inspirational and practical advice, have helped the thousands of people who have tuned in to my podcasts. They have found a renewed sense of inner strength and purpose, spiritual wisdom and, ultimately, their passion for life. And each one of them continues to share so that others can find their own way forward.

As these wonderful thought-provoking writers began submitting their chapters for *Good to the Last Drop!*, their stories seemed to naturally form themselves into three distinct stages:

Part 1: Grief and Rebirth

Part 2: Embracing Life, Reinvention, and New Purpose

Part 3: Living Your Best Life

In Part 1, you'll read the stories of several authors, me included, whose lives were rocked to the core by life-changing events: the sudden death of my husband Saul in a car accident; the tragic death of Casey

Gauntt's promising young adult son Jimmy; and, the cancer journey of Angela Clement's husband Blaine and his subsequent passing. In their stories, you will feel their aching pain and grief and read about their gradual emotional rebirth as they communicate with their loved ones who have moved to another plane of existence. You'll also read about Yvonne Heath's life as a single mother raising her children and coming to realize that she is the only one who can control her life, her feelings, and her actions. Ellie Pechet then shares her difficult family history that led to years of childhood physical and emotional abuse. Despite it all, she fanned a flame of hope and, as she entered her twenties, began a long journey of healing and discovery of her true calling, which she continues to practice now, well into her sixties. And finally, you'll read about Mark Ireland, who lost his beloved teenage son Brandon. Mark worked through his wrenching grief and went on to help found the worldwide parental support group Helping Parents Heal. Over the years, he has identified five pillars of healing from grief that everyone reading this book will find positive, supportive, and encouraging.

Part 2 examines the various ways the authors came to find new, renewed purpose or added clarity in their lives, whether from personal loss and trauma, epiphany, or the recognition of the need for supports for those experiencing loss. For example, Julie Lazar-Reskakis found during her nursing career and later work as a bereavement specialist that the medical world needed to provide bereavement support to families who had lost a fetus or baby shortly after birth. Although retired, she became a certified perinatal bereavement specialist and volunteered to set up a hospital program plus two others, which she runs to this day.

After losing her mother to a terminal illness, Phyllis Okon reinvented herself as a multi-published fiction author and publisher at age fifty-eight, even as her husband was succumbing to cancer. After his passing, she trained to become a medium and has felt her husband's encouragement from beyond as she, in turn, helps others connect with their spirituality.

Betty Jampel reinvented herself after a long career as a therapist and social worker. At an age when many think of retirement, Betty has become a specialist in healing people's spirits through non-ordinary states of consciousness. Betty works daily with terminally ill patients and firmly believes that the healing approaches used by Indigenous peoples throughout history can and do help us today to see our interconnectedness in a "core unity of consciousness."

Jeff Rasley realized the importance of finding a balance between solitude and community after a night lost on a mountain in the Himalayas. That experience taught him the importance of community and social connection as being an integral part of our humanity.

Alan Stein has been living with metastatic cancers most of his adult life. Despite this and an abusive childhood upbringing, he has maintained a positive outlook and, now in his seventies, has embraced his third chapter and is still actively involved in a variety of business and philanthropic pursuits.

After the passing of his 15-year-old daughter Shayna, Brian Smith was devastated. It took him some three years to work through his grief, but he kept believing that there is meaning in everything that happens to us. He joined Helping Parents Heal and has become a best-selling author, counsellor, and podcaster.

During her traumatic youth, Tami Hendrix found comfort with animals. When she was plunged into despair with the sudden passing of her sister, she turned to her dogs Murphy and Snoopy for comfort and later Katie, while continuing to work and raise her family. Through animals, she found her calling as a healer and has forged a strong connection to her spirit and her soul.

In the weeks following the passing of her mother, Julie Ryan developed a deeper understanding of the spiritual dimensions of life and death. Julie believes the experiences she and her family had in the hours leading up to her mother's passing were her mother's final gift.

Part 3 presents the stories of contributors who are still living their best lives well into their sixties, seventies, and eighties. Faust Ruggiero lost his mother early in his life. Her passing left him determined to make a difference in the lives around him and he promised himself to honor her memory by reaching out to help others. Through his counselling work, research, empowerment books, and podcast, he continues to live a life of love and service to humanity.

Now in her seventies, Francis Rae Key continues to share her love of music and peace with the world. But back in 2010, she lost her mother and experienced the greatest loss of her life. Soon after, she received messages from her mother's spirit and wrote four books based on messages from a team of spirits. To find out what happened next, read her chapter!

Roz Weinberger freely admits she has "attitude". But, she's found her feisty attitude combined with a smile and laughter has successfully carried her through many life challenges. Also in her seventies, she is a personal trainer, a potter, and a property manager. Busy lady!

Mary Metcalfe is a childhood trauma and cancer survivor. After decades of depression and anxiety, she was finally diagnosed with Complex PTSD in late 2018. After a period of grieving the COMPLETE loss of contact with her daughter and two grandchildren, Mary has moved forward with "an attitude of gratitude" for life's lessons and found renewed passion and purpose as she enters her seventies. Now in his late eighties, Bob Wells had a lengthy career as a wildlife conservation officer and was married for sixty-two years before his beloved wife passed on from Alzheimer's. Following a massive heart attack, Bob now uses a wheelchair and stays on top of climate change issues. He holds monthly "talking circles" with fellow seniors at his long-term care home to encourage them to stay engaged and involved in living their best lives.

Mark Pitstick offers his eight insights into growing older with grace and purpose. This is one chapter you'll return to again and again!

When Anita Albright lost her beloved daughter, her entire world changed. Through her deep grief, she had to come back into life. She embarked on a mindfulness journey that helped her reconnect to life without her daughter. But first, she had to embrace Grief. In doing so, she learned much about herself and her ever-present connection to the universe.

Heidi Connolly's husband passed on in 2012, leaving her mired in grief. Her husband's spirit reached out to her from beyond and helped her see that life was worth living again. She now sees life as full of choices for her to make and trusts her intuition to remain in alignment with life.

In the final chapter of this book, Mary D'Agostino leads us through the heart-wrenching loss of her youngest son in an accident. She realized that part of her healing involved taking care of her own physical and spiritual needs with kindness, compassion, trust, and feeling. At each step along her healing journey of awareness and love, she met her true self. And, as she reminds us, "Life is just beginning. Again."

The challenges and trauma these writers have faced often trigger a period of intense grieving and introspection, which can and did alter their outlook on life, faith in themselves, humanity, a quite dynamic spirit world, and our belief that there can ever be better days ahead. But once they explored their new reality, they realized there *is* something more. There *is* a way forward to better days.

As you read the stories in *Good to the Last Drop!* you will be challenged to see grief and aging in a new light. Seen from the perspective of living your best life to the best of your interests and abilities, *Good to the Last Drop!* is a call to life and living. These are stories about great loss and life-altering challenges, yes, but they are also living proof that the worst of times can, with support, care, and encouragement, gradually be transformed into a hopeful and positive future.

My greatest hope for *Good to the Last Drop!* is that it will support you in opening your mind to healing from deep emotional pain, whether caused by trauma or loss or both. With the support of proven effective approaches to your healing, you will begin to recognize possibilities to find new joy, fulfillment, and meaning in your life that will lead you to a renewed sense of passion and purpose.

It's never too late to live your life *Good to the Last Drop!* and engage in living each day with love, kindness, compassion, and respect for yourself and all life.

Irene Weinberg

West Orange, New Jersey
March 2024

PART 1

GRIEF AND REBIRTH

*"The reality is that you will grieve forever.
You will not 'get over' the loss of a loved one;
you will learn to live with it."*

—Elisabeth Kubler-Ross

*"We never lose our loved ones.
They accompany us; they don't disappear from our lives.
We are merely in different rooms."*

—Paulo Coelho

MY CELEBRATION OF LIFE!
~ IRENE WEINBERG ~

ON DECEMBER 21, 1997, my life abruptly changed course when my beloved husband Saul left this earthly plane after we were in a tragic car accident. I had known in my soul that his passing was coming and, as he died beside me that night, I knew with certainty that our journey together was far from over. In the last months before Saul passed on, I had received three very clear messages:

- Saul has to go. Many lessons will be learned from his death.
- He's not going to make it. You are.
- Be loving and kind to everyone.

That night in 1997 changed my life in so many ways. I lost my husband on this physical plane, but gained a loving and trusted spirit guide who is with me daily and who has influenced my thinking and actions in more ways than I can ever count. Out of my devastating loss, pain, and grief, I began a healing journey that continues to this day. In the process, I learned more about myself and discovered an inner strength and resiliency I continue to build on with each challenge life throws up to me. I also rebuilt my passion for life and use it to be of service to humanity even as I approach my eighties.

As another chapter author in this book wrote, "You're never too old to be part of the solution." I choose to dedicate the third chapter of my life to "loving more deeply and living more happily," in the words of Saul as he communicated them to me for my first book, *They Serve Bagels in Heaven*.

In that book, I explored with Saul the meaning of eternal love, the kind of love that transcends every religion and embraces all cultures and beliefs. The kind of love that connects and interconnects every entity on Earth, the kind of love that requires acceptance of that truth. I learned that love is a behavior – it is "an action of respect for those around you."

After the accident, I began working with a Life Transition Coach, who encouraged me to find new interests as a now alone woman. Soon after I came out with *They Serve Bagels in Heaven*, I was invited to attend a Future Search Conference that was focused on creating peer support services for children who were grieving deceased parents, grandparents, and siblings. I became a Founding Board member of what became a non-profit called Good Grief, and served in that organization on a volunteer basis for seven years. Although I've been out of Good Grief now for about twelve years, it was heartwarming recently to hear from someone that her grieving grandchildren, whose father died of pancreatic cancer on New Year's Eve, are going to be going to peer support at an organization called Good Grief. What I helped to create helped me, it lives on, and it continues to help countless grieving children.

I know from my own research that some older people find themselves wondering what happens when you have lived a good life and don't know what to do next. To my way of thinking, finding meaning and purpose is essential to finding joy and happiness as we age. Finding meaning and purpose are the keys to building resilience as we age and face the inevitable challenges of our advancing years. With resilience, comes empowerment. That sense that no matter what life throws at you, you have the patience, knowledge, tools and networks to lean in to life's challenges, secure in the knowledge that you *can* make a difference.

At some point, after living our best life, we will let go of our earthly physical presence and join the spirit world. I know from my own experiences, that this transition to another plane of existence is something to look forward to and nothing to fear. As anyone who knows me will tell you, I don't plan to go with a whimper. In fact, quite the opposite.

A longtime friend recently said that she is sure my family will give me the traditional Jewish Memorial Service, but she'd love if there was also a celebration of my very full and "colorful" life after the traditional Memorial Service. She wants to deliver an irreverent and fun eulogy about me. When I mentioned this to another friend, she chimed in, "I want to eulogize you next!" I have been friends with Laura and Betty for over twenty years. We all love celebrating life, and I *love* giving parties. So, one day I felt inspired, started thinking about what kind of party I would plan, and went for it!

At some point, I mentioned the party and eulogies idea to my son, and he said, "Mom, if you create it, it will be done!" And now I am having great fun creating a party that will be a celebration of my life after my bodily demise! I think it will be a great way for my grandsons to know more about their 'Gaga' and maybe even tell some stories of their own! It will be, in every sense that Brian Smith notes in his chapter, a "graduation" party as I transition from my earthly life to the next stage of my evolution. My challenging life has taught me many important lessons, so I consider it my graduation party from this very challenging school called LIFE!

I've created a Word document with instructions for the party to take place in my condo and I assured my son that Saul and I, and my mom (Grandma) will definitely be there! *We wouldn't miss it!*

Since most of my friends are younger than I am, I'm hoping that they will be at the party (I prepared a guest list), as well as family members and anyone else my son wishes to include. I even told my son which of my friends' fave foods and drinks to be sure to provide at the party, and to keep those glasses filled! I also told him to please place balloons throughout the condo to add to the fun party atmosphere, and to have special bags created that say: "Your gift, with love always from Irene!" so my friends can place their Irene keepsakes in their special bags!

Why special bags? Since I have already left certain personal items to family members and friends in my will, I decided to ask my son to open my jewelry boxes and closet to the party goers so that they can take home "pieces of Irene" that they want to use with joy, to enjoy the memories.

In my new document, I have even added both my toast to be read by my son to my beloved friends and family members, before he turns the party over to the two "keynote speakers" followed by anyone else who also wants to add their comments, and my closing remarks to be read at the conclusion of the party.

And I instructed that all items not chosen are to be donated to the local battered women's service, because it was there that I began to understand my natal family dysfunction in a new light, which aided my lifelong healing journey.

Now all I have to do is to enjoy adding to the stories that will be told at the Celebration of my life during this "third chapter" of my life and continue adding details to the Celebration document when they occur to me. And I must add, not only am I having fun creating this party, because I love creating wonderful fun gatherings, but it is also surprising me because it is bringing me much peace and closure throughout the process!

For now, however, I am busy engaging with life and living, through my interviews with people from all walks of life who have overcome trauma, tragedy, and grief. Many of them are finding new passion and purpose as they grow into their Third Chapter.

Someone said that retirement is not about stopping, it's about shifting gears, so you keep moving forward. I can certainly not only live with that, I'm embracing it!

THE LETTER

~ CASEY GAUNTT ~

I SAT IN MY law office on a sunny November, 2008, morning in San Diego, California, but the bright day couldn't raise my spirits. Three months earlier I'd lost my 24-year-old son Jimmy. After partying with some friends, he decided to walk home. He never made it. In the darkness, on a narrow, winding, road, a car struck him. Not enough time for either to avoid the collision —nobody's fault. Just a terrible accident.

A knock on the door roused me. Shelley, my assistant, entered as if she were walking on eggshells. "An Emily Sue Buckberry called. Said you were both in Coalwood, West Virginia, many years ago. She has something you left behind and thought you might want it. Here's her cell number." She laid the pink phone slip on my desk and left.

I certainly remembered Coalwood. I'd spent the summer after high school graduation working at the Olga Coal Company. My father's Chicago-based company, Case Foundation, was contracted to punch a 2,000-foot ventilation shaft into a new section of the mine, and my dad, Grover Gauntt, sent me to work there before I started college in the fall.

If you read Homer Hickam's bestselling memoir, *Rocket Boys*, or saw the 1998 movie, *October Sky*, you might recognize "Coalwood." This Appalachian miners' camp near the Kentucky border is where Hickam grew up and started his high school rocket club that won the National Science Fair Grand Prize Medal in 1960.

I arrived in Coalwood in June 1968 and quickly learned that almost everything was owned by the company, including the Clubhouse, a three-story white boarding house run by Junior and Carol Chapin. I settled into my second-floor room, eager to begin work the next day.

> *I was consumed with a feeling, a deep knowing, that something very strange and exceptionally powerful was afoot.*

The job site was two miles down Snakeroot Hollow, in a place called Mudhole. The job ran three shifts per day. The work was hard and dangerous. I learned to drill holes in solid rock with a sixty-pound jackhammer and pack the holes with dynamite. The first time I used the tamping rod, I was terrified.

After setting the charges, we'd be hoisted out of the hole. The fire master would holler, "Fire in the hole!" and press the hot button. The ground shuddered underfoot. Then the sound rolled out of the shaft like Thor's fury after one of Loki's tricks. When the smoke and gases cleared out, a mechanical mucker would scoop up most of the rock. The rest we'd shovel out by hand. On a good day, all three shifts would advance the shaft about ten feet.

As the son of the Case boss man, I was viewed with suspicion. Someone even searched my room, trying to find out what this silver-spoon boy was doing in Coalwood. As time went on, my willingness to work hard earned me respect and friendship.

I learned a lot of things in Coalwood. In addition to operating an air-powered drill with a six-foot diamond-tipped bit attached, and stuffing fuses into sticks of dynamite, I learned how to test for methane gas, the chief nemesis of all coal miners. I also became adept at chewing tobacco, smoking unfiltered Camel cigarettes, shooting rats with a .22 rifle at the local garbage dump, and drinking 3.2 beer and an occasional snort of homemade moonshine.

I also made a lot of friends both on the job and with other boys who lived in town. They honored me with an invitation to play on their softball team that played other nearby mining towns. Although I was extremely apprehensive about spending a summer in a place unlike any other I'd ever been, it turned out to be one of the most memorable and enjoyable periods of my life.

In late August, I flew off to the University of Southern California in Los Angeles, where I majored in business and law and met the love of my life, Hilary. As far as I was concerned, Coalwood was forever in my rearview mirror.

Now, forty years later, a voice from the past had caught up with me. The Buckberry name meant nothing to me, and I hesitated to return the call. What could she possibly have of mine that I would want? After considering the message for an hour, I dialed her cell phone.

"Emily Buckberry," a staticky voice said.

"Uh, this is Casey Gauntt. You left a message for me?"

"Hey, Casey. You probably don't remember me, but my mom and I lived on the third floor of the Clubhouse the summer you worked in Coalwood." Her voice was effusive and gregarious.

She was right. I didn't remember her.

"You used to play your guitar on the porch and sing. Sometimes we'd all sing along."

An image of long brown hair and a smile hovered in my mind.

"When you left Coalwood, I was bummed that I didn't get to say goodbye. I went past your room and saw a letter and an empty Case Foundation envelope addressed to you lying next to a wastebasket. I picked them up and scanned the first couple of paragraphs. Your father had written about problems the company was having on the Olga job, and I was afraid that if that got around town there'd be big problems.

"So, I kept it, intending to send it on to you. But I got sidetracked with graduate school and life in general. The other day, I was going through some boxes and found the letter. I googled you, called your San Diego office, and here we are."

Yes, we were.

She chattered on. "So, Casey, are you married?"

"Yes," I grunted, anticipating her next question.

"Any kids?"

"We have a daughter, Brittany." Tears welled as I told her how Jimmy had died only three months before. I barely heard her words of condolence.

All of the laughter and light-heartedness was sucked out of her voice. She was stunned and, for once, at a loss for words. Finally, she asked me, "Do you want the letter?"

I managed to give her my home address and hung up. Instantly, my body was awash in goosebumps from head to toe, and I felt like a current of electricity was pulsating through me. I'd never before experienced anything like it. I was consumed with a feeling, a deep knowing, that something very strange and exceptionally powerful was afoot.

Two years after that summer in Coalwood, I'd flown home to Chicago for Christmas. Dad was away on a business trip, but he was supposed to return the next day. I woke up that morning to find my little sister, Laura, on my bed, shaking and crying. Mom stood in the doorway, her face ashen. "They found your father in his office this morning. He shot himself."

While I had lived the college life and hung out with my fraternity brothers, the company was consumed with financial problems. A deep recession mired Case Foundation in debt. On top of that, the developer of a massive Chicago skyscraper, the John Hancock Building, had filed a $100 million lawsuit against Case and my dad for alleged faulty foundation work. Dad became more and more frustrated, exhausted, and depressed, until he finally gave up.

On Christmas Eve day, a letter addressed to me arrived. Inside were three hundred-dollar bills and a one-line note scrawled by Dad: "Please get something for your mother and Laura for Christmas." Stricken, I handed Mom the money and tossed his note in the trash. Two weeks later, Mom packed up the house and moved to her folks' place in California. I went back to college.

Emily and I didn't talk about my father during our call or how I'd spent the better part of the last four decades trying to bury his memory and all of the pain and suffering he'd brought upon me and his family. He was supposed to keep us safe. Instead, he abandoned us and ruined our lives. I did my best to keep my own family secure and happy and shield them from hurt. But I couldn't keep Jimmy safe.

On the Saturday after Emily's call, Hilary and I went with our daughter, her husband of one year, Ryan, and my mother to Del Mar Beach. The Santa Ana winds had blown in a perfect day: cloudless sky, a sea the color of sapphires, and temperatures in the high seventies. Brittany and I paddled past the surf line on boogie boards and spread some of Jimmy's ashes. Around three o'clock, Mom wanted to go home, while the others stayed at the beach.

I dropped Mom off and decided to swing by our house and check the mail. Inside the box was a priority mail package from Emily. I took it inside and tossed it on the counter. There it lay while I fiddled around the kitchen for a bit. What could be in it? Would it bring back even more terrible memories to see my father's handwriting — knowing that he had only two short years to live before leaving us forever?

At last, I tore the strip off the package and pulled out the Case Foundation envelope. The envelope was postmarked June 19, 1968. I drew out the letter. Dad's neat handwriting spread across both sides of the page. Phrases jumped out at me. "We have lost a lot of time on the job . . . leadership a big factor . . . good contract, but it doesn't cover stupidity . . . your leadership qualities might be contagious . . ."

He revealed a depression in his youth, his insecurity, his religious zealot of a mother, and a war that changed him.

More phrases. "I'm not going to preach to you. Should you want and ask for my advice, I'll give it . . . don't expect you to follow it blindly . . . only you control your destiny."

Nothing in the letter was familiar to me. I looked at the envelope. It was in pristine condition, as if it had been steamed open. I always tear the top or side of an envelope to get to a letter. Always. That letter never got to me that summer in Coalwood.

He closed his letter with this: "I'll be around, any time you want me. I'll be there, because I care more than you'll ever know, my son. All love, Dad."

My body shook with sobs. I turned to look for him – and Jimmy. I felt my father was in the kitchen with me. And what I didn't mention is that Saturday, the day the letter finally arrived in my hands, was Jimmy's twenty-fifth birthday. *His letter arrived on my son's birthday.* My father knew this day would be one of the hardest days of my life, and he was here with me, as he promised.

Postscript

The letter from my father arriving all those years later, on the day it did, was a game-changer for me and my family. I instantly realized my father never stopped watching over me and loving me. I discovered there is something much bigger and more powerful around us than I ever imagined. Instead of running away from him, I began to run to my father and learn everything I could about him, and why he wrote about those things he suffered as a child and young man. I began to properly mourn his death.

I also knew this miracle was meant to be shared. I wrote the story and gave it to my family, our friends, and Jimmy's friends. Thus began my transition in my early sixties from a hard-charging corporate attorney to my second and most rewarding career as an author, speaker, and grief advisor.

I started a blog in 2011, www.writemesomethingbeautiful.com, and in 2013 co-founded a group, The Fraternity, of fathers of children who have transitioned. In 2015, I published a book, *Suffering Is the Only Honest Work*, that features this story "The Letter." My second book, *When the Veil Comes Down*, came out in 2021. One of its chapters is "Healing with History." I found that looking deep into my past and the struggles of my ancestors helped me with healing in the present. In early 2022, I pulled together *The Gauntt-Case Clans*, a compilation of stories I've written about my family's roots and some of its more colorful characters. And in early 2023, I came out with the first biography of legendary dam builder, and good friend of my grandparents, *Harvey Slocum: Best Dam Man In the World*. More about the books can be found at www.caseygaunt.com.

Hilary, my wife and best friend for over fifty years, is a passionate cook and hosts a very popular food blog she started in 2011: www.heronearth.com.

I thought my life was over after our son was accidentally killed, and I harbored dark thoughts that my father was somehow responsible. However, they both reached through to save me, and showed me the door to the Third Chapter of my life: one filled with a new sense of purpose to help others suffer less, explore the incredible mysteries of existence on both sides of the veil, and a deep knowing that love is eternal.

AWAKENING THROUGH GRIEF
～ ANGELA CLEMENT ～

MY HUSBAND, BLAINE was my best friend, my partner for thirty-five years, and the love of my life. We owned a cattle ranch north of Val Marie, Saskatchewan in Canada, gateway to Grasslands National Park. It was the perfect place to raise our two beautiful children. I was the principal at the school in Val Marie. In 2019, with our children off on their own, my husband and I made a big decision to sell Clement Ranch. We were ready for retirement. I planned to retire within the next few years. We had plans to camp every summer at our seasonal spot in the Cypress Hills and travel in the winter. We eventually would move to a larger center, follow our children, and look forward to being grandparents one day.

In January 2021, Blaine wasn't feeling well, and he went to the doctor. I was at work the day he got the results and he put me on speakerphone to hear from the doctor. I fully expected it to be a gallbladder issue or a hernia, but it turned out to be colon cancer. The next ten months were a like a dreadful nightmare. In February, I took leave from my position at Val Marie School so that I could look after Blaine. He started chemotherapy, which made him very sick, and he was in and out of the hospital between the nausea, all the blood tests, and bi-weekly treatments.

In April, we purchased a home and moved to Maple Creek where we could be closer to a hospital, my son Curtise, and my daughter-in-law, Jennifer. Shortly after we moved, Sheldon, my daughter Whitney's fiancé, received a lymphoma diagnosis. We spent the summer running for treatment. At least twice, Blaine and Sheldon were in the hospital at the same time to receive their cancer treatments. I couldn't imagine that it all could happen at once. In August, we had to put our beautiful Australian Shepherd dog to rest as he also had a tumor in his colon.

> "People will tell you that you will grieve for a lifetime. I choose otherwise. I choose the path from hurt to hope, to healing every day."
> —Julie Cluff

In September, my son-in-law finished his treatments, and we celebrated a clean scan. It truly was the bright spot in that year. Early in the morning of October 25th, I woke up to my husband showing signs of confusion and increased weakness. My daughter-in-law, Jennifer, who is a nurse, suggested that we may not have much time left. We arranged for a J-P to marry Whitney and Sheldon in our home so that Blaine could witness the marriage. That same afternoon, my son Curtise and his wife Jennifer announced to Blaine, and me, they were expecting a baby. Blaine could congratulate Jennifer and Curtise and responded to the wedding with a clap over his head. We were truly so thankful for that. After the wedding was over, we called the ambulance and took Blaine to the hospital. He passed away the next afternoon on October 26th, one day shy of his fifty-sixth birthday. I became a widow and my whole life changed.

> I believe our grief journey is uniquely and beautifully designed for our healing. If we look at grief as a helpful friend for healing rather than something to be avoided, it will show us the way back to joy and happiness.

I had developed a keen interest in energy healing ever since my son was healed of Hirschsprung's Disease by a healer named Roxene Harris. I read books on the subject over the years, and would dabble in healing and practice on others when I could find a little time between being a wife, mom, and educator. While Blaine was sick, I was increasing my knowledge and practice of energy healing to help us get through the physical and emotional turmoil. I did sessions with Blaine every day and had two other healers working with him as well. I believe that is the reason I was able to keep him at home until the day before he died and why he took very little pain medication until just a few days before his death. When he passed away, it seemed natural I would continue to take more classes in energy healing. I also signed up for sessions with a grief coach.

Writing became a way for me to express what I was going through. Sharing my story through a blog I created was benefiting others as well. I took a six-month online energy healing course with celebrity healer Adrien Blackwell starting in January 2022. I achieved the status of Reiki Master and, in addition, Adrien introduced me to several other healing modalities. As part of a marketing portion of the course, she also taught me how to create and host an online summit. This would be the beginning of a series on grief titled "Awaken Your Soul's Journey".

In my first summit, I interviewed twenty-seven experts in the field. Despite my initial fear and nervousness about sharing my experiences, hosting the online summit turned out to be a positive opportunity for me. I learned more about grief and established a supportive community. Upon the completion of that summit, I took a grief certification course from my coach, Julie Cluff. I held another summit in the fall and started an online support group. I also did one-on-one healing and grief coaching.

When I wasn't focusing on my healing or helping others, I was travelling. In February 2022, I visited my aunt and uncle in Mesa, Arizona. I also spent a week in Sedona on a healing retreat in the hills, trying different techniques like sound healing, breathwork, and shamanic practices. In March, my mother and I had the opportunity to travel to Europe. We enjoyed a river cruise down the Rhine with Energy Healer Donna Eden and her husband, David Feinstein. They held workshops on the ship where I learned more about Eden Energy Medicine and Energy Psychology. I was also able to go on a trip to South America for a cruise around Cape Horn with my parents. My whole life I have dreamed of seeing penguins and it was magical to get to walk amongst them in their natural habitat. I went on a trip to Costa Rica with my friend Gail who was also a school principal from just down the road who, unfortunately, had also become a widow. I found travel healing for me.

Since Blaine transitioned, I have become a grandmother twice. My grandson, Benson Blaine, was born on June 16th, 2022. My granddaughter, Sierra Whitney, was born May 25th, 2023. They are the source of great joy for me. I spend time with them often.

Many people wonder how I have been able to move forward from my grief. It did not start out easy, but little by little, I found my way. Refusing to believe what so many say about grieving for a lifetime, I followed my heart and let it guide me through the healing process. I found a quote on Facebook by Julie Cluff: "People will tell you that you will grieve for a lifetime. I choose otherwise. I choose the path from hurt to hope, to healing every day." One never knows what small message is going to make all the difference in the healing journey. This really resonated with me for one big reason. I was looking for hope. I use what I've learned to help others find HOPE (Heart Opening to Purpose and Expansion) and live a passionate, joyful, and purposeful life.

I credit Blaine and my guides for connecting me with the ideal healers, teachers, and support. All I needed to do was be brave enough to say yes to it all. It became an opportunity for me to awaken to who I truly am and discover my purpose here in this life. I experienced challenging days where I thought I wouldn't survive, but I learned to let the waves of grief wash over me. I believe our grief journey is uniquely and beautifully designed for our healing. If we look at grief as a helpful friend for healing rather than something to be avoided, it will show us the way back to joy and happiness.

Through the loss of my husband, devastating as that was, I have begun a journey to find myself. The Angela I am now was not possible before. I am taking what I have learned from my beautiful, loving life with Blaine and using it to propel me forward into this new life. No matter where life takes me, I know he is right here with me every step of the way. He is cheering me on and loving me still. I feel his essence all around me. It is a special relationship, uniquely ours, that continues until the end of time because a love like this never dies. I cherish all the beauty and magic from my memories, and they fuel me to become more and more who I am ultimately here to be. My future is full of possibility nourished by my past.

WITNESSED

~ SHIRLEY LYSTER ~

THERE IS GREAT truth to the concept that telling your story over and over is a way to process and understand events that don't make any sense when they happen. The pieces are everywhere when your world explodes, and it is in speaking out loud that you call those shards back and put them into a semblance of order. Your story, and you, evolve over time and retelling.

The greatest gift that can be given is to be witnessed in your grief as you puzzle out the story. It gives the sense that you and your story are heard. Being seen as you truly are in those moments of pain and suffering allows you to begin to comprehend the unimaginable that has happened to you. There are two parts to my unimaginable – chronic illness and death.

"Mom, there's blood when I go to the bathroom."

One event can change the course of your entire life. It was a beautiful June day in 2016 and my youngest son, Cam, was home for a visit. He'd gone across the country to attend college and while there, began working as an Army Reservist. He loved the military life so much that he'd left college to work full time for them. This visit was his last free time before he went to Basic Training and began his military career in earnest.

We were on a road trip, our favorite thing to do together. The music had been played and we'd done our catching up. The car had always been an intimate space for my sons to talk to me and he chose that time to drop this bombshell. He promised me that if it were still happening after Basic, he'd see a doctor, but he really didn't have time to do it before. It's come to me now that he didn't want anything health-related to affect his chances with the military.

Fast forward to the beginning of December. The bleeding and other symptoms had intensified, and his doctor ordered a colonoscopy. The procedure confirmed that he had developed pancolitis, the most severe form of ulcerative colitis. It is the inflammation of the entire large intestine due to an autoimmune response to attack the intestinal lining. His guts were seen as the enemy by his body. Symptoms can range from blood and mucous in the stool, to severe fatigue, excessive urges to vacate the bowels, anemia, and a host of other symptoms that vary from person to person. There is no known cause and no cure. As with all autoimmune diseases, nothing works for everyone, and it is a long course of trying various medications with the hope that the next one will be the magic bullet that makes the bleeding stop and the pain go away.

Our family had been extremely fortunate in that none of us had ever been sick or hospitalized. We knew nothing of the toll a severe diagnosis takes on a person and the people around them. Ulcerative colitis wasn't in our world, and all of us were ignorant of the severity of the diagnosis. This was our crash course into the world of chronic illness. Every spare moment I had I was online, researching and trying to figure out how I could help my son. I was the mother who oversaw all the minutiae of our family life. I could

The person I vowed to protect when he was born was the one that I could do nothing for.

tackle anything, but this was beyond my mere mortal capabilities, and I was frantic. The person I vowed to protect when he was born was the one that I could do nothing for.

I absorbed all I could about the disease and its cohort, Crohn's disease. What I learned horrified me. These diseases are insidious and totally take over a person's existence. My fun-loving, adventuresome boy was housebound across the country, alone with his pain and suffering. As his disease progressed and he couldn't work for the military any longer, he made the decision to release and come home to be taken care of. Needless to say, I researched even more so that I could give my son the care that he was going to need. I knew it was going to be life-changing for us to have him home, unaware of what the fates had in store for us.

I moved Cam home on March 12, 2017. The trip had taken its toll on him, and he was exhausted. To this day, I don't know if it was that trip that was the beginning of the end, but I know it had been excruciating for him. A mere week later, he passed on in our home of a perforated bowel with me at his side. The anguish, anger, and feelings of helplessness were the catalyst for catapulting me into my third chapter.

Those feelings are powerful forces and can get things accomplished if channeled appropriately and, in those hours and days afterwards, I had so many unanswered questions about his treatment and this disease. I vowed to do my best to make sure this didn't happen to someone else. My resolve strengthened as the long months without my son rolled by. What could I do to ensure his death wasn't swept under the carpet? How could I enlighten others, so they weren't as ignorant of this prevalent disease as we were? It was through my research that I found out the horrifying statistics of IBD (Inflammatory Bowel Diseases – not to be confused with Irritable Bowel Syndrome, a cluster of uncomfortable symptoms that do not damage the digestive system) in our country. Canada has the highest rate of diagnosis in the world and the provinces Cam lived in have the highest incidence in the country.

Young adults and children have the highest diagnosis rate of these horrible diseases. But what could one person do?

The easiest thing to do and, it turns out, the best thing I could've done, was to sign up for the local chapter of Crohn's and Colitis Canada. It was there that I found my voice. The development coordinators for the city and the region were both very receptive to Cam's story and insisted that it was one that people needed to hear. They sent our story to the national coordinator and soon I was contacted by their social media department. I could feel the heartfelt understanding in all my interactions with these caring individuals who themselves lived with the disease or had loved ones that endured it. I felt seen, heard, and understood.

With my permission, Cam's story was used for their national fundraising campaign. I was so impressed with the care and attention they paid to every detail. They added photos and took great care to match the font to the style the Canadian Forces uses in their correspondence. You see, these campaigns usually rely on the feel-good stories of how an individual has overcome devastating illness to live their best life managing the disease. This time, they wanted people to know that there are tragedies involved with this diagnosis and not everyone has a happy ending. It was a beautiful tribute to my son. The mailout campaign aligned with my national interview by their social media coordinator, who lived with the same diagnosis as Cam. We went through the entire story from beginning to end to try to bring a firsthand, intimate feel to the mailout. I had achieved my goal of informing the entire country of how serious these diseases could be in a noticeably brief time!

That wasn't good enough though because I knew that the people who are the most likely to be diagnosed were not reading the mail and certainly not watching a Crohn's and Colitis interview. My career as an Education Assistant enabled me to speak to the 15-16-year-olds in our building about the diseases. It took "guts" for Cam to tell me that he saw blood in the bathroom before having any pain. I was certain many children and young adults would shy away from that conversation, so I wanted them to know that it's imperative that medical care is received as soon as possible. I know that Cam waited too long after the first incident to get help.

To lighten the topic, the focus is on "Poop" the emoji. They've been receptive and have listened intently, especially knowing that they or one of their friends could be diagnosed. In tandem, I hosted an annual dodgeball tournament (Cam's all-time favorite physical education sport!) for the high school, which is anticipated more than anything else! There are poop-themed prizes for every team participating, door prizes, and a Guess the Candy Jar. It runs for a week during lunch break and has become a school tradition. Learning needs to be fun to get the point driven home and I feel better knowing that there are ambassadors out there now who will understand and be compassionate to people diagnosed not only with IBD, but any debilitating illness.

My storytelling began within that first year. I wrote it, I spoke it, and reprocessed every detail. With every telling, I'd catch something I'd missed, something that I'd misplaced, and things that I'd imagined. The mind needs life to be orderly and if it's not, will make up details to get the end result it needs for a tidy package. Even now, I go back to what I knew six years ago and catch inconsistencies but that's not something I do very often. I try extremely hard to not look back because I'm not going that way.

> By going public, by going out of my comfort zone, I opened myself to compassion from strangers and friends alike.

What I have realized is that by giving the interviews, by allowing Cam's story to be used for the mailout, and by speaking to the students every year, I have been witnessed. My pain was seen and held by so many people in my community and across the country who understood what I felt in those months, whether they'd lost someone to the disease or lost the person they'd been prior to diagnosis. People who had never experienced child loss knew that I was living their worst nightmare and while they didn't understand the full impact, tried their best to show me grace while I grieved. By going public, by going out of my comfort zone, I opened myself to compassion from strangers and friends alike.

I also concluded that even though I felt held and understood by those people, it wasn't a place I wanted to stay. It would've been more comfortable to make the choice to stay in my grief. British author and philosopher Alan Watts said, "There is never anything but the present, and if one cannot live there, one cannot live anywhere." To crawl out of the crater Cam's illness and death left behind and force myself to enter the world again was a conscious decision. I needed to get back into the present. The past was a dark place that I couldn't live in anymore and so I forced myself to go back to work part-time, against the advice of family, my doctor, and the Human Resources department. I worked with children and there is nothing like children to make a person feel alive again.

I never felt I was betraying Cam's memory by re-entering the human race. What I felt was that I had a reason and a purpose for telling his and my story. We don't stop mothering when they pass on and even though I couldn't mother Cam in this life anymore, I could take care of others. I channeled the energy and love I needed to give my son into my presentations and speeches. Their story becomes an innate part of who we are and my last third of this life has changed to encompass the people who suffer from IBD and their families. My circle of love has widened to include them, and I know Cam would be so proud.

DECADES OF LEARNING TO LOVE MY LIFE TO DEATH

∾ YVONNE HEATH ∾

HAVE YOU EVER wondered what happened to your life when you were suddenly forced to make a U-turn or change lanes when you thought you were going in the right direction? Me too! I loved being the fixer, the go-to person, strong, and independent. I often pretended I was fine when I wasn't, drowned and buried my sorrow with red wine and suffered excessively. Can you relate?

The good news is that from my deepest despair came my greatest strength – *real* strength, not the pretend kind. From my greatest challenges, the very best version of me was born: my flawed, imperfect, and fabulous self. And she continues to learn, unlearn, and evolve every day. She often fails and tries again. Ok, that's enough third person talk. Allow me to introduce myself – through the decades.

Early Life

My name is Yvonne Francoise Marie Heath, born on February 16, 1965 on a cold Canadian winter day to a terrified young woman who planned to give me up for adoption – believing this would give me a better life. Everything changed when she held me for the first time. She didn't know how she would manage but chose to be my mom. I am forever grateful for that. In the sixties, nice Catholic girls did not get pregnant. Imagine the guilt and shame she felt and I absorbed for years. I only began to understand the impact much later in my life. I had to let go of feeling responsible for all my mother went through. I tried to "fix" her and diminish the pain I felt I caused for so long.

As a little girl, I was loved but never felt like I truly belonged, like an outsider in my own family. Then there was teenagerhood: puberty, cramps, pimples, weight gain, mean girls – I was always trying to fit in. Never quite getting there. Rebelling without even knowing why. I made it through, though not unscathed. Did you feel insecure and carry it with you? Yeah, me too. Well, the twenties would be so much better . . . right?

Lessons Learned

- *Everyone has their journey. It is not up to us to judge, fix, or change it.*
- *We can both bury and carry our childhood experiences. There is much to learn. Dig in.*

Twenties

As many young women do, I *thought* I knew almost everything and proved myself wrong time and time again. I went into nursing school not knowing what else to do. I knew I loved helping people. Looking back, I realize it also helped to 'make up' for the pain I'd caused and to avoid dealing with my own issues. I craved love but constantly attracted rejection into my life. After one particularly humiliating breakup, I packed up my car and became a traveling nurse. I left Canada and moved to Louisiana and then Texas. I learned the two-step, what chicken-fried steak was and saw just how big belt buckles could be! I thought I could escape rejection by being so far away. The problem is that wherever you go, there you are. I just kept *looking for love in all the wrong places* and getting dumped over and over again.

After falling for a navy boy, my life changed forever. I became pregnant. I was in love with the idea of being in love and having a family. I ignored the signs, red flags, and drinking. Tyler was born on December 17, 1993, my beautiful boy with jet black hair and a pouty face. I became a new person. I was a mom, and I wanted to give my son a good life! The rose-colored glasses came off. I knew one day the two of us would have to leave.

Lessons Learned

- Our denial can run deep and we can be quite convincing when we want to paint a pretty picture. Forgive yourself, learn, and do it differently next time.
- We can be angry for the way people treat us. However, they can't treat us this way without our permission. Sorry for the tough love! (I learned that the hard way!)

Thirties

I accepted that I had married someone who was consumed by alcoholism who had no desire to change. It felt unbearable, and I had to leave. Divorcing and moving back home with my toddler to live in my parents' basement was certainly not on my vision board. I was broke, broken, and lost. I remember announcing when I lived in the US, "Mom, you might as well accept that I will never again live where there is snow!"

And here I was back in northern Ontario with lots of snow! *Eating your words . . .* is that the expression?

As I wondered what had happened to my life and how to fix it, I sought out counsellors and mentors. I searched inside for answers instead of blaming my external circumstances for where I had landed. It took a long time, but eventually things were heading in the right direction. I was finally behind the wheel again.

I began to forgive myself for things I wished I had done differently. I decided I would not settle for anything less than what I really wanted. I deserved that. Tyler needed a mom who cared about herself. That's when I met Geordie, the love of my life. And thank goodness for therapy because I almost walked away from this amazing relationship because he was *too nice.* That was not familiar. How sad! It started as innocent flirting; after all, he was over thirteen years younger than me! Obviously, it wasn't going to be serious. But we sure did have fun together. In fact, we had so much fun, we married on September 20, 2003! Woohoo!

Lessons Learned

- *If you're ready to love yourself and others, love can find you – even in a small town in northern Ontario.*
- *Whatever you are going through is temporary.*
- *You never know what awaits on the other side of grief.*

Forties

Twenty days before my fortieth birthday, I delivered our twins, Jadyn and Tanner. It was the most frightening, amazing, and fulfilling time. From the past fragments and fractures I created a whole new life. My family was finally complete. The Heath Family Five. Life was good. I was a nurse in a chemotherapy clinic, married to my soulmate, with three children living in beautiful Muskoka, Canada. We were happy. Until we weren't.

Tyler had many challenges: abandonment by his biological father, our years of being on our own, struggles in school with ADHD (like his mom), and bullies. His outlet and passion was snowboarding but a serious knee injury landed him on the sidelines in pain. This was the breaking point. He was crushed and spiraled down into a dangerous world of alcohol and drugs. Watching helplessly nearly destroyed me. We sought help everywhere we could and eventually admitted him to a rehabilitation center. Imagine the anguish I felt as a mom. My soul throbbed. He said we saved his life. It was a long journey. After rehab, Tyler seemed to be in a better place. He eventually settled in Kelowna, British Columbia, surrounded by mountains. He is still on that rollercoaster, and we support him in every way we can.

On this devastating path, a painful realization was some people were there for us while many disappeared in our time of crisis, when we needed them most. I also felt obligated to be strong, handle it, pretend I was fine when I wasn't, and to check my personal life at the door when I went to work – in a hospital where, ironically, we take care of people. I shouldn't make people feel uncomfortable, right? This added to my suffering and feeling isolated. I couldn't imagine at the time it would be the catalyst for a life-changing movement! I became more anxious in a society that didn't allow for hard conversations. I asked other healthcare professionals, "Are we well prepared for grief, death, and dying?" The response, "Oh no we're terrible at it." And off they went.

I wondered who was teaching communities and professionals to normalize these conversations – throughout life? Nobody.

Then one day, I saw a pop-up on Facebook, "How to write a bestselling book" and it knocked me out of my chair. "That's it! I'm going to leave my 27-year nursing career and write a book!" And with no experience or know-how, that's just what I did. It wasn't a logical decision but I didn't have a choice. Passion and purpose were in the driver's seat now. I was just along for the ride!

Lessons Learned

- *No matter how hard we try or how much we want to, we cannot control anyone but ourselves.*
- *Some have harder journeys than others. Don't get stuck in "Why."*
- *When people don't know what to do or say, they may avoid – afraid to do or say the wrong thing and make it worse.*
- *Sometimes when we discover a problem and look for someone to help with the solution, the only person we find is in the mirror!*
- *Listen to your Inner Wisdom. It knows the way.*

Fifties

What a surprising decade! If anyone had told my younger self this is who I would choose to become at this stage of my life I would have laughed hysterically and assured them they had me confused with someone else. I did not see any of this coming. And now I see that every challenge, crisis, disappointment, and heartache led me to exactly who I was meant to be.

Hello, my name is Yvonne Heath – former nurse turned author, speaker, trainer, and changemaker! I had no idea how far out of my comfort zone I was going to leap. Thank goodness because I would have done a quick 180-degree turn. Being naïve was my saving grace!

As I continued to write, five decades of feelings, witnessing gut-wrenching pain, being silenced with *that's just the way it is,* and pretending poured out onto the pages. I needed more. I sent out one email that changed everything. I asked if anyone would be willing to tell me about being in the deep trenches of grief, getting to the other side, supporting loved ones as they died, working in healthcare, etc. Would anyone be brave enough? I didn't think I'd get any replies. I sent that email in 2014 and guess what? The stories haven't stopped coming!

To this day, I am corralled in the grocery store to hear about a son's addiction, an email about holding a loved one's hand as they took their last breath, a student who was acting out and no one knew how to support them after their dad died, and on and on. More than anything, people wanted and needed to be heard; to have a safe space to share their story. And their stories lit passion and purpose within me. I was always goofy and silly but never wanted the spotlight to share a valuable message . . . until now. I had to vacate my comfort zone permanently, feel the fear, and do it anyway.

I began sharing my message before my book came out with my flipchart and markers. I became a guest on podcasts and remember being asked for my media kit. "Of course, no problem!" I said I'd send it then immediately yelled to Geordie in the other room, "Honey, google *what is a media kit?*" He did and we created it. We learned along the way – one step forward, three steps back. And just kept going. When my mentor said he would ask a producer about me hosting a television show I giggled to myself with a "Yeah right, as if that's going to happen." When the response was an enthusiastic yes, I had to stop myself from either fainting or crying. I was trembling as I agreed and wondered what I had gotten myself into? And why? Why would I do this to myself? Right . . . passion and purpose had overtaken logic.

My book was launched in 2015. We've sold thousands of copies and continuously receive messages of how it has changed lives and perspectives on death. I still pinch myself and am so grateful I was chosen for this. I've hosted two television shows, a radio show and even delivered my TEDx Talk – *Transforming our Grief, by Just Showing Up*. The greatest parts are the incredible people and organizations I've had the privilege to work with and learn from.

We can have heartache, trauma, excruciating grief and get stuck in it forever. Sadly, this is the end of the story for so many. Or . . . we can acknowledge and allow all of our feelings *and* create something good from our experience. How? By sharing our story and creating a life we love again. We can show what is possible and help heal ourselves and others.

It is a privilege to be a voice for so many who have not been heard. Their spirit and grit guide and inspire me. I continue to learn, unlearn, and evolve. I finally love my whole self – flawed, imperfect, and fabulous. I embrace being a silver-haired fox. I've earned every line on my face and accept the cellulite, broken veins, and progressive sagging. I do find the rogue chin hairs offensive. What's up with that? Another opportunity to laugh, that's what. We can navigate this journey we call life with heart, humor and humanness. We can allow the grief and joy to co-exist – no matter what we are going through.

From pain to purpose,
I chose to be the change I wanted to see and founded:
Love Your Life to Death and the *I Just Showed Up* Movement –

Teaching people how to *Just Show Up*

For themselves and others
so they are empowered and resilient
when grief arrives.

I LOVE this third chapter, the life I am creating, and the person I have chosen to become. It has been a journey fraught with U-turns, dead ends, roundabouts, and many curves. But I persevered. I will continue to share what I've learned – in my sixties, seventies, eighties, and beyond. I will fail and try again and again. That's the very best we can do.

Lessons Learned

- Be Proactive. Practice. Teach by Example.
- Carry Love and Gratitude with you, wherever you go.
- When you don't know what to do or say, Just Show Up with Heart, Humor and Humanness.

And my final call to Action:

>Plan Your Life, Plan your Death, then just . . .

>Love Your Life to Death.

And always . . . bring your own tambourine to the party!

DEVELOPING COMPASSION THROUGH TRAUMA
~ ELLIE PECHET ~

WHEN I WAS first asked to contribute a submission to *Good to the Last Drop!* I wondered how I was going to be able to formulate into words my vast experiences of pain turned into growth. It seemed like a daunting task but one I am being guided to do as an inspiration to others, who will hopefully be inspired to keep going . . . no matter how challenging life can be at times.

My parents grew up in Romania during the Holocaust. Although they were not in concentration camps, they were significantly traumatized by the Nazi culture, what they witnessed and experienced, and how they were treated because they were Jewish. They lived in fear daily, and this went on for years. I remember my father telling me how humiliating it was as a boy having to wear a large Jewish star made from cloth that had to be sewn into their clothing to identify them as Jewish . . . as if they had done something wrong just because of the religion they were. He was beaten up by other boys and ridiculed because he was Jewish.

My mother was a shouter for the most part when I was growing up and although she didn't talk much about her experiences growing up in the hostile anti-Jewish culture, she had many scars that she carried forward for the rest of her life as a result. For example, I remember when I was growing up it seemed like she was always extremely concerned about all issues having to do with security. She needed to have an alarm system in every house we lived in and was very concerned about the status of the doors and windows, whether they were open or closed, unlocked or locked, etc. She didn't give me my own house key until I was a young teenager and a lot of it had to do with her needing to feel safe and able to have control over things that could make her feel vulnerable such as keys and access to the house.

The wounds my parents carried with them from the Holocaust were deep and vast and there was a lot of darkness in the home I grew up in to say the least. They married and immigrated to the United States in the 1950s and in that period, psychiatrists and counselors were only for "sick people" and those who couldn't handle their problems, so my folks didn't get the support or the help they needed after the traumatic experiences they endured during the Nazi era.

As a therapist, I know now that they each had untreated Complex PTSD from what they experienced in the Holocaust. This condition then developed in me due to the environment I was subjected to growing up. Back then, however, the attitude was to have a stiff upper lip and keep moving forward. The emphasis was on survival, making a living, and not much else. In a sense, I would say that they brought a piece of the Holocaust with them when they moved to the United States and that darkness filled my home and influenced the vast majority of my experiences growing up.

I was by nature, a sensitive, empathic kid, and a natural observer. I was curious about people, and it was natural for me to observe everyone and everything around me. From a metaphysical perspective as I look back, my deep knowing is that I came into my family of origin as a vessel of light to bring light into the darkness that existed. My mission, although I didn't know it until much later, was to help my parents and two sisters in their own evolution by being a messenger of light.

It did not go as I hoped or intended when I made the plan and agreement before I incarnated into physical form in the sense that I don't think I was able to help my family of origin evolve. In fact, it was a very long, tough, uphill battle . . . I remember often wishing I was grown up so I could be out of the hell I was living in. The emotional, spiritual, and physical pain was so great and so constant, if I had to pick one word to best describe my childhood, it would be *torture*.

> I remember often wishing I was grown up so I could be out of the hell I was living in.

My existence growing up was lonely. I had no ally. My parents came to the United States just the two of them, so growing up, there were no relatives to offer support. Once every year or two, we would visit our relatives in Venezuela, where the rest of our family had settled. My maternal grandmother intuitively/energetically pressed the dormant, intuitive button within me when I was only two or three years old on one of her few visits with us in the U.S.

I remember standing at the top of the stairs in our home in Massachusetts. She was at the bottom of the stairs when she opened my third eye. This was done without words, as an energetic act she initiated. She was the only one in the family who had the gift of intuition and recognized that in me as well. After that activation, I was able to see and feel negative entities and had chronic nightmares, which is one of the symptoms of not only PTSD, but also that negative entities may be present. Identifying and removing negative entities eventually became one of my specialties and I wrote a book about it as a service to humankind to help people understand entities are real and do exist.

I am sure my parents came from the Holocaust atmosphere with negative entities . . . how could they not? The Holocaust was one of the darkest times of human civilization and there were countless dark entities and demons present, influencing not only Hitler, but the vast majority of Nazi soldiers who carried out heinous acts against so many people during that period.

My folks didn't like feeling like I was observing them. I wasn't doing it on purpose, it was my nature to be more of a quiet observer as I mentioned earlier. My intuitive sense is it bothered them because of the darkness they carried within from their past and their unprocessed secrets. It's likely they knew I could sense the darkness within them and didn't want to be reminded of it.

I was hit, pummeled, and pushed to the floor on a regular basis. I remember one time I was in so much emotional pain I couldn't bear it anymore and started shouting at my parents who were in the living room, from the top of the stairs. My mother sent my father upstairs to "quiet me down," which was their way of silencing me and silencing any needs I had. In other words, he hit me until I stopped. The analogy I think of when these events/beatings happened is that of a flower that wilts without care, sunshine, and water.

Emotional abuse and neglect: one of the most damaging ways my parents and sisters scapegoated me was by blaming me for anything and everything that went wrong in the family. I remember listening outside the door as my mother would coach my younger sister not to be like me or act like me in any way, shape, or form. Not only was it very hurtful to hear these words and made me feel like I was bad and defective, my sister took advantage by also torturing me in her own way, one of which was to hide items that belonged to me and deny it. I remember one time I had been working at a bagel shop and saved up to buy a moped that looked like a motorcycle. I absolutely loved it, and it was my pride and joy, a treasure I had acquired for myself through my own efforts. One evening, soon after, my sister got her best friend and her brother to come by and steal it. I remember that morning when I discovered my moped was missing, I was supposed to take my SAT exams. I was so upset it was very difficult to concentrate on the exams. She completely denied it and our mother believed her as usual. To this day, she has never admitted her role in getting my beloved moped stolen.

How was I able to survive and transform such a traumatic upbringing to do so much good in the world?

First, even though it certainly felt like my family of origin came close to snuffing out my light they didn't succeed. Probably, the biggest lesson I learned because of my own suffering as a child and teenager was that I developed deep compassion for others who are suffering. Hence, my life calling and mission to become a healer and meta-physician and to serve so many with my ability to heal and ease their suffering.

When I was in my twenties, I began my personal healing journey, starting with counseling. I also felt very drawn to the spiritual aspect of things and started exploring my intuition and spiritual healing in the form of various types of energy work. I wanted to understand what I had been through from a spiritual perspective, intuitively knowing this would at least help me make sense of my experiences growing up. Little did I know consciously that my upbringing would significantly influence my mission and work in the world this lifetime. It would not have been possible to develop as deep a sense of compassion and understanding of the suffering people can endure without having gone through what I did in my own life.

As I ventured forward on my path of healing my past, by way of counseling, spiritual growth, and energy healing, I realized the combination of all three resonated deeply for me. Eventually, these three approaches evolved into the remote healing practice I offer my clients to this day.

The spiritual side of things has always made so much sense to me, not only for my own journey, but it has always been a big part of my approach with my clients. Look at it this way:

The counseling helped me understand, process, and receive support, and the energy work helped dissolve the energetic charge of the pain, thus accelerating my overall healing.

in this current life, there is the 'little us' in the here and now, experiencing and reacting or responding to what happens in our life. There is also the 'big us' – complex and expansive. It goes beyond this current life and includes all our past lives. I believe that the older the soul is, the more advanced and the more difficult the lessons tend to become. When we are willing to swim with the current of our soul's journey, it helps our soul advance. If we lean into the lessons we are assigned in this life, as uncomfortable as they usually are, we reap the benefits and rewards of knowing we are on track not only by growing as a human and as a soul, but also with our mission here on the earth plane.

Some people go through their entire lives wondering what their calling is and searching for it, trying different vocations. The younger sister I referred to earlier has had at least four different occupations. I am glad to have found my calling this time around early on, in my twenties, because I have been able to help so many people over the decades.

Currently, I mostly work remotely with clients, which helps make it possible for anyone to access my healing anywhere in the world. I also heal clients' family members and pets simply by working with their photo and obtaining some basic information such as name, age, symptoms, etc.

In recent years, my healing abilities have accelerated, and part of my calling has developed into extending my remote healing practice by helping specific groups of wildlife as I feel called intuitively. Some wildlife groups I have worked with remotely in recent years have included elephants in Africa, numerous groups of wildlife affected by the wildfires in Australia in recent years, and the whales in both the Atlantic and the Pacific to name a few. I have also done specific cleaning sessions for our oceans, all of which are recorded in journals with each healing. I do my best to maintain a sense of balance while helping human and pet clients, as well as wildlife projects as I am called to do so. Although up to now, I continue to do remote work with wildlife as a service, it is my hope and vision that the importance of this aspect of my work will be recognized and that there will be those individuals who want to financially support this branch of my work.

Sometimes I *astro travel* to where I am most needed while my physical body is sleeping, such as a place that has experienced some kind of disaster. For example, right after the nuclear disaster in Fukushima, I felt called to help and astro traveled there, energetically working with people who had been exposed to radiation from the nuclear disaster. Eventually, I had to stop because astro traveling long distance night after night was wearing me out and I started to get sick.

By transitioning from my experience of being victimized during my upbringing to creating and living a fulfilling life on purpose with my calling, I want to share with those who are reading my story and may still be suffering, that even though it might seem insurmountable at times to transcend the pain and grief, it is doable.

Here's to your personal healing on the human level, along with your growth and evolution as a soul. No matter what you have experienced and no matter how much pain you have suffered or are still suffering, know that you are loved, you are lovable, and you can heal much more quickly than you realize.

> *Even though it might seem insurmountable at times to transcend the pain and grief, it is doable.*

THE FIVE PILLARS OF HEALING GRIEF
~ MARK IRELAND ~

STARTING IN 2008, I spent a good deal of time promoting my first book, *Soul Shift: Finding Where the Dead Go,* at bookstores, in media interviews, and at various workshops. It was in the latter of these, a workshop in January 2010, that I met Susanne Wilson. A gifted Medium, Susanne, would serve a crucial role in connecting me with Elizabeth Boisson. At the time, I had no idea how significant this meeting would be.

My inspiration for writing the first book was tied to the unexpected and wrenching passing of my youngest son, Brandon. Then eighteen years old, Brandon was climbing the McDowell Mountains behind our Scottsdale, Arizona home when something went wrong. He passed out and never woke up again, at least in a physical sense.

The varied remarkable experiences that transpired after Brandon's passing became the foundation for the book. I documented these phenomena as extraordinary cases of connection with my son, facilitated both directly and through Mediums. These experiences were not only touching and healing, but they also delivered irrefutable evidence of life after death – the continuity of Brandon's consciousness and personality. I knew that I had to share my story with others who were suffering through loss.

Unlike most people, relying solely on blind faith for hope in a spiritual dimension – the afterlife – my life has been filled with direct evidence of this reality. My father, Richard Ireland, was a prominent psychic medium and minister, who counseled people from all walks of life. From common everyday people to celebrities like Mae West and Glenn Ford, to the Eisenhower family, he served many and gave them hope.

On countless occasions, I saw my father demonstrate psychic phenomena and spirit communication, where specific indisputable evidence was furnished. I had a first-hand view of how these messages brought hope and joy to grieving people. So, from a young age, I knew that we are more than just a physical body and a brain. I came to understand that we are a soul or spirit temporarily experiencing life in a physical body.

> *From a young age, I knew that we are more than just a physical body and a brain. I came to understand that we are a soul or spirit temporarily experiencing life in a physical body.*

Despite this childhood knowledge and the comfort that it brought, I sought a different path than my father, focusing on career goals in the business world. That is, until Brandon's passing, when I was jolted back into a profound spiritual search, re-entering my father's field with a sincere yet grounded spirit of inquiry.

Returning to the workshop, and my chat with Susanne Wilson, I learned that she'd recently relocated from Florida to Arizona and attended the event to meet like-minded people. She told me that she was an experienced medium and to provide evidence, delivered some amusing and accurate validations that clearly came from my deceased uncle and father.

During our chat, Susanne mentioned that she was seeking an office where she could bring clients. The landlord, a woman named Angie Bayliss, who owned a yoga studio, was unfamiliar with mediumship and asked for proof of Susanne's abilities. Not wanting to risk having an unscrupulous person as a tenant, Angie challenged Susanne with a test.

Susanne asked Angie for a picture that she could "read". Angie took a holiday card that she had just received from Elizabeth Boisson out of a desk drawer, handed it to Susanne, and asked what she could share about it. The photo on the card featured three young people – two females and one male, who, unbeknownst to Susanne, were children of studio client Elizabeth Boisson. The male in the photo was Elizabeth's son, Morgan, who had passed from altitude sickness while on a university trip to Mount Everest.

Despite knowing nothing about the people on the card, Susanne began delivering numerous validations about Morgan. Since Angie didn't know if any of the information was correct, she later met with Elizabeth to review the statements to assess their accuracy. As it turned out, Susanne was not only uncannily accurate but the details she furnished were immensely significant and meaningful to Elizabeth.

Susanne didn't mention specifics about this reading with me during the workshop – I learned of them later on. She just stated that she'd recently connected with a woman who'd lost a son on a mountain. Feeling a sense of compassion, I handed Susanne a signed copy of *Soul Shift*, along with my contact information, and asked her to share them with the young man's mother.

Just a day or two later, I received a call from Elizabeth, who said she'd read my book in one sitting, loved it, and wanted to meet my wife and me.

Within the week, Elizabeth and I connected in person and immediately hit it off. She told me that she'd started a Facebook support group called Parents United in Loss. Elizabeth went on to say that she was about to hold her first in-person group meeting and wanted me to serve as the inaugural speaker. I gladly agreed. The first meeting went well and Elizabeth continued having monthly meetings.

Fast forward to November 2011. I was leaving a corporate job and thinking about what I should do next. My friend Tina Powers, an exceptional Medium, said, "Mark, I think your main mission in life is to help other parents who've been through the same thing as you. Maybe you could create an organization focused on that."

After digesting Tina's words, I knew what she said was true and that I should find a way to serve in the way she'd suggested. But then I started thinking about Elizabeth's group, noting that it had been very effective in assisting grieving parents; I concluded that there was no need to "reinvent the wheel". I wondered what might happen if Elizabeth's process was blueprinted and replicated in affiliate groups across the U.S. and possibly beyond. The only other missing elements were a website and a monthly newsletter.

So, I called Elizabeth with a proposition, asking if she'd like to partner in creating something bigger to serve more people in many locations, noting that I'd be happy to set up a website and newsletter. She immediately said, "Yes, let's do it." I then proposed an alternate name, "Helping Parents Heal". Elizabeth responded, "Yes, I love that name and am not happy with the name "Parents United in Loss".

Thus it was that Helping Parents Heal (HPH) was born – the next version of what Elizabeth had established in 2009. Several of the original members from Elizabeth's group became founding members of HPH and subsequently, some of them joined the board once the organization was incorporated.

The key differentiator between HPH and other parental support groups is that the organization encourages the open discussion of spiritual experiences and afterlife evidence. This is done in a non-dogmatic way, as people from all backgrounds are welcomed, whether religious or not. HPH is not affiliated with any religious denomination.

Today, HPH is operationally directed by Elizabeth Boisson, President, and Irene Vouvalides, Vice President. These two dedicated individuals work with our affiliates, coordinate meetings and Zoom presentations, and manage all aspects of our conferences. It's a very big job and a full-time endeavor for them both. I currently serve HPH as Board Chair – a far less demanding oversight role.

The organization now has more than 26,000 members, and over 175 affiliate groups worldwide, and provides frequent Zoom presentations with renowned speakers. HPH also hosts a conference every other year, organized by Elizabeth who serves as Conference Director, with support from Irene Vouvalides, and a group of parent volunteers. Our second conference, in 2022, drew nine hundred attendees, filling the hotel to capacity in what proved to be an extraordinarily healing event. I attended the conference and presented, but it was Elizabeth, Irene, and a cadre of volunteers who planned and executed everything.

Hotel employees were concerned about hosting a group of grieving parents, assuming that the atmosphere might be depressing. On the contrary, the energy was very high. The hotel associates told us that HPH was the best group they'd ever had.

With that backdrop, I'd like to wrap up by sharing some things I've learned about the healing process. At HPH meetings, I've seen people come in for the first time who were in a state of deep depression and/or overwhelming sadness. Later, a metamorphic process seemed to take place with many of them, where they shifted from despair to a state of contentment and even joy. These folks became "shining light parents", a moniker shared by Suzanne Giesemann and adopted by Elizabeth, Irene, and the organization on the whole. During my observations, I assessed the reasons for such transformations and decided to share what I call the "Five Pillars of Healing Grief". I'm not saying this is the only list, as there are surely many more things, such as therapy, that can help people heal. But these five points tie to what I've personally observed:

1. *Support from family and friends*: Not everyone has the luxury of a supporting family and group of friends, but when one does it can be very helpful. Oftentimes, people close to the grieving parent won't know what to say; they may offer platitudes that aren't helpful. Friends and family may also be uncomfortable talking about the child who passed and will sometimes try to change subjects or avoid the topic altogether. Most parents I know in this situa-

tion want to talk about their child and they find such discussions helpful and healing. Family members need to understand what the bereaved parent needs and wants during this time, so they can provide support in the best manner possible.

2. *Meeting other people who've experienced the passing of a child*: Getting to know and befriending others who have been through the same thing can be very helpful. They can fully relate to you because they experienced the same thing and understand what it feels like. Such relationships allow people to provide mutual support to each other. Helping Parents Heal provides an opportunity for parents who've had a child pass to meet others in the same situation, through in-person meetings and conferences.

3. *Service:* When a person is ready, they should consider doing something positive that is of service to others. This could be working at a soup kitchen, donating time to a non-profit organization, setting up a foundation to raise funds for a worthwhile cause, establishing an HPH affiliate chapter, or anything else constituting service to others. When you help others, it comes back to you and provides healing.

4. *Release of guilt and learning to forgive*: Many parents blame themselves in some way for the passing of their child. They will think or say, "I should have done this", "I should have done that", or "I should've seen the signs". The reality is that most parents bear no responsibility for the passing of their child and couldn't have changed the outcome. They need to let go of the "what if" kind of

> *Most parents bear no responsibility for the passing of their child and couldn't have changed the outcome. They need to let go of the "what if" kind of thinking and release self-imposed guilt.*

thinking and release self-imposed guilt. Likewise, some parents harbor deep anger toward another person who may be in some way responsible for the passing of their child. Whether an accident or something else, it's not easy to forgive, but the person who is hurt the most is the one choosing not to forgive.

5. *Openness to afterlife evidence*: Read books about NDEs (near-death experiences), mediumship, death-bed visions, and other phenomena providing evidence of life after physical death. Consider learning meditation techniques to facilitate a direct connection with the child that passed, or possibly a reading from a vetted evidential medium. This evidence is the *hope* element that differentiates HPH from other organizations of its type.

To assist with the fifth pillar of healing, I created a Medium Certification program in 2014, testing Mediums under controlled conditions. Mediums are required to participate in five readings conducted via Zoom, with no video, where they don't know the sitter, and must generate statistically significant results for accuracy, pertinence, and specificity. Today, about forty such Mediums are featured at https://www.findacertifiedmedium.com

And while it is the fifth pillar that brings the hope element, all five are important for a balanced healing approach. I don't want people to become medium addicts.

If you've suffered the pain of having someone close to you pass, I encourage you to connect with a group that provides support to assist with the healing process. Your life has meaning, you have a purpose and gifts to share with the world. So, hang in there and work through this – it will be worth it in the end!

PART 2

EMBRACING LIFE, REINVENTION, AND NEW PURPOSE

"Death ends a life, but not our relationship, our love, or our hope."

—David Kessler

"It takes strength to make your way through grief, to grab hold of life and let it pull you forward."

—Patti Davis

MY JOURNEY FROM AUDIOLOGIST TO PERINATAL BEREAVEMENT SPECIALIST, AND A FEW THINGS IN BETWEEN

JULIE LAZAR-RESKAKIS

AS MY SENIOR year in high school approached, my father handed me a directory of colleges to use as a guide to research what I would do next. It was the seventies, there was no Internet to browse, and virtual campus tours did not exist. Up to that point, I had not given much thought to where I wanted to go. This was a time before kids began preparation for college in grade school. I opened the book to page one and never got to page two. Sure, Alfred University, that would work, and it did for four wonderful years. I graduated with a Bachelor of Science in Psychology, however, at that time there were very few viable options for employment. I quickly realized that continuing my education would be essential to continue in my chosen field.

Due to unforeseen circumstances, I had to postpone graduate school for several years. When it was time to get serious about continuing my education, I went back to the trusted college guidebook I had used previously. Again, I never got past page one. Sure, Adelphi

University, that would work, and it did for the next three years. At that point I had begun to question if psychology was really what I wanted to continue pursuing, so I looked at a list of careers. You guessed it, I never got past page one! Sure, a Master's in Audiology, that would work, and it did, for thirty-five years.

Much of my time as an audiologist was spent working in nursing homes. I had an affinity for working with the elderly and would spend as much time holding their hands and listening to their stories as I would testing their hearing and fixing their broken hearing aids. Around that time, the administration at the nursing home began to scrutinize billing, time spent per patient, and staff productivity. Luckily for the patients, a closed door was necessary for accurate audiological testing (and storytelling).

During the years I spent working in nursing homes, I recognized that there was a need for more support at the end of life. The facility where I was employed for many years opened a ten-bed hospice unit. There were not many referrals for an audiologist on the hospice unit given the other more immediate concerns for their patients. I was called to the hospice unit only once to fix a broken hearing aid. However, when I could, I would visit the unit to talk to the staff who worked there. I was interested in the hospice philosophy and curious about staff roles and patient care. During this time, a seed was planted to possibly pursue hospice volunteer work when I retired, but that was still some years away.

Shortly after I retired, I saw a posting for a three-day End of Life Doula training workshop at a local hospice. I was interested and signed up for the program. Upon receiving my certification, I began volunteering at the hospice several days a week. The volunteer aspect worked well with my retired lifestyle as it offered extensive flexibility. I was, and still am, part of a team of volunteers and doulas, dedicated to helping people live out their final days and months in as much of a meaningful and peaceful way as possible. I continue to be passionate about this work, despite the inevitable sadness that often comes along with it.

About five years into my doula work, I became interested in helping to support families after their loved ones had died. An amazing bereavement counselor at the hospice took me under her wing. An opportunity to become a Certified Grief Educator came along and I was excited to obtain this additional training. This was an inaugural program offered by David Kessler, an accomplished author and one of the world's most highly recognized grief experts. I completed the training and became certified in this new specialty. I have continued my volunteer work at the hospice in this role, co-leading bereavement groups while also participating in patient visits.

Several years later, as I regularly did, I was listening to Irene Weinberg's *Grief and Rebirth* podcast. I valued the wisdom and knowledge that Irene and her guests provided. Irene's guest that day was Sherokee Ilse, a perinatal bereavement expert. I was in my car driving a long stretch of the New York State Thruway and from the moment Sherokee began speaking I felt as if she was sitting next to me in my car. As the time and the miles flew by, I was mesmerized.

At the end of the podcast, Sherokee shared her cell phone number and I reached out to her. We talked for some time and our conversation affirmed to me that this is the work I wanted to do. I knew that this was going to be the next chapter in my life. I had my own history of pregnancy loss many years earlier and did not receive the support I so desperately needed at that time. I wanted to change that narrative for other families.

> I had my own history of pregnancy loss many years earlier and did not receive the support I so desperately needed at that time. I wanted to change that narrative for other families.

I trained with Sherokee Ilse for seven months online and in person in Pittsburgh. She is a pioneer in the field of perinatal bereavement, a recognized author of many books on the subject, and an internationally known speaker. Although there were other training programs available, I knew Sherokee's was the gold standard. In 2022, I became the first person certified by Sherokee in the state of New Jersey. To my delight and honor, she has become a dear friend, and we have worked together on several projects.

Upon becoming certified as a Perinatal Bereavement Specialist, I contacted my local hospital with a proposal to begin a program there. The goals were to support families through perinatal loss and help them honor their babies by spending the short amount of time they have together making precious memories. I was met with enthusiasm by the hospital administration and hired as a member of the Labor & Delivery Team in 2022.

I recently launched two new programs in the hospital supporting women and their families through early pregnancy loss in the Emergency Department and on the Same Day Surgery Unit. All families need and deserve to receive the best possible support during such a difficult time, and I am working to ensure that the length of the pregnancy does not dictate the level of bereavement support.

Thank you, Irene Weinberg and Sherokee Ilse, who helped me find my way. Irene's amazing *Grief and Rebirth* podcast, coupled with Sherokee's knowledge and wisdom, sent me on this path.

I am eternally grateful.

MOTHER OF REINVENTION
PHYLLIS OKON

MY KIDS HAVE a nickname for me. They call me the Mother of Reinvention. I have to begin by saying they get indignant when I call them my kids. I work with them, they are my partners, business colleagues, and ages forty and forty-five respectively. We share a family business. They have worked hard beside my husband David and myself for many years, and now serve the company as President and COO.

This is a firm that my husband and I founded in a kitchen with a twelve-hundred-dollar loan from my kid brother close to fifty years ago. I was working as a substitute teacher when my husband asked me to join him and run the back office. I wanted to teach social studies but full-time teaching jobs were scarce. My husband spoke with a heavy accent, and writing anything in English was difficult for him. He needed help to run the business and asked me to step in and build something new and exciting.

My parents were horrified. *Who uses chauffeured car service?* they asked. Certainly no one in our circle of friends and family. I wasn't worried. I trusted him and agreed as long as we could start a family, and our work life together began.

I knew nothing about car service, and while he could fix anything with a motor, David had little knowledge about business either. He handed me the *Yellow Pages,* opened it to car services, and told me, "*Call them and ask what to do.*"

These were times before the Internet. I ordered a stack of phone books and began with limousine services, soon graduating to cold-calling other types of businesses to get work.

I buried myself in learning how to optimize the cars. Within a few years, I handled reservations, dispatching, billing, payroll, account receivables, payables, recruitment, sales, and licensing. I was up at night to guide the last car in and awake at daybreak to get the first one out.

David fixed the cars, bought and sold them as they aged, kept the drivers in line, and drove clients. He also shared household responsibilities, as well as parenting, at our home. We each did what we excelled at, working as a team. I never asked for a paycheck or a title. The business belonged to him, and I was content to take the backseat. It was never an issue.

No one was more surprised than me as the business grew. It was like our noses were so pressed to the grindstone we never saw it coming. One day we looked up and realized we had a fleet of cars that supported many people, a reputation to be proud of, and enough money to expand our business beyond our wildest dreams. Soon my parents, my brother, and my ex-sister-in-law worked alongside us creating a perfect dream team.

David was always the boss and I was happy for him. He provided me with what I wanted, and I returned the favor.

We named my mom the comptroller. She reveled in her title, elevated for the first time in her life from the role of bookkeeper. She was brilliant, clever, sweet, and my best friend. When she was diagnosed with lung cancer and lost to us within two years, I felt the rug pulled out from under me.

It had been a tough few years. Both my mom and husband were diagnosed with the same disease within three months of each other with my partner and best friend, one terminal, the other promising he would make it through the narrow eye of the needle to survive.

Either way, it rocked my neat little world, and I sank into a depression. My sons saw my lack of spirit and encouraged me to write. This had been a lifelong dream that was often derailed by other pressing matters.

The business always took precedence; taking care of my desperately ill husband and keeping all the nuts and bolts of our lives running smoothly filled all my time. Good things occurred too, happy events that must be acknowledged and celebrated. Both of my sons' lives evolved. They moved out, got married, and started having children. Life kept recalibrating.

But my life had altered, and I wasn't happy with myself. I felt like I lost my anchor.

My sons urged me to re-find and redefine myself. It manifested into a literary career at fifty-eight where I became a de facto representative of retirees reinventing themselves in the independent publishing world.

It spawned a self-help book, a magazine, a podcast, and countless interviews and articles about this journey. I've been interviewed by *Forbes* twice. I joined a community of Indie writers, helping them with advice and encouragement.

I ended up publishing over seventy-five books, many of them award-winning. A script is being developed and shopped in Hollywood based on one of my novels. A joke book I wrote outsold every book on Amazon for over two months during the pandemic.

I delved into the marketing end, taking control of my older son's novels. I learned how to promote and market our books, adding another skill to my repertoire. It was fun and exciting. It kept me fresh, relevant, and connected with a wide group of people I might never have met.

However, my husband, my greatest advocate, started to fail. The eye of the needle was closing. He was brave and strong and never complained. He fought his

> *No matter how prepared you think you are, you never are.*

way to the end, refusing to let cancer beat him, but it was one battle he couldn't win. It was over in a blink that left me reeling.

No matter how prepared you think you are, you never are.

That brings me to today. He's been gone almost six years now. As his widow, I stepped into his formidable shoes. I am now the CEO of our company. *Me*, who rarely held a title and worked behind the scenes.

I miss him. I spent forty-eight years working beside him, every day of our lives. We talked and supported each other through everything. He was my sounding board, and I needed his frank advice.

As successful as I had been with the writing, I found a certain dismissal of me as a CEO by my peers. The view from this end of the desk is disheartening. Why do I have to be recognized as a *female* CEO, when men are simply referred to as the CEO? *Why do I sense an impression that others think I fell into this job?*

Reinvention time, again, but not just for me. I had to change the world's perception around me. This is not ego speaking. It's born from a deep sense of wrongness in our culture.

My husband and I set the tone in our business to respect individuals based on their accomplishments, not judge them on their age, race, creed, or gender. The result has been a wonderful diversity that makes our company stronger.

It was never more apparent than when my sons named two women as directors and were approached by their male counterparts who complained about promotions due to political correctness. Without blinking an eye, my younger son responded, "No, they were promoted because they do a better job than you."

Still, I missed my husband's input. I wanted to hear what he thought about my decisions. I went to countless mediums looking for answers. We went to mediums for years, communicating with family that had crossed over. In fact, we prepared for his departure with a special message that was promptly delivered at my first session.

When COVID hit, I did Zoom sessions with mediums from all over the world. There seemed to be a common message in each of the readings. *You can do this yourself, try. You'll be good at it.*

Reinvention time again.

I started with one class and soon was moving from teacher to teacher, learning, reading, attempting to do what they do, see what they see.

I knew my husband was helping me from his side. I could feel it.

In a mentorship class of eighty-six people, I was the only one the teacher endorsed.

My sons, ever the cheerleaders, created a podcast during the pandemic, invited me on, and threw me to the wolves.

Without telling me, they brought on a willing subject for me to read. And I did. Successfully.

I learned I could do this.

Reinvention works.

Rediscovery, stepping outside my comfort zone, and learning that my horizon is unlimited is inspiring. You're never too old to try something new. You might even see it through different eyes. Life's experiences make us stronger, smarter, and more perceptive.

> You're never too old to try something new. You might even see it through different eyes. Life's experiences make us stronger, smarter, and more perceptive.

I will be sixty-nine when this book is published.

The big number is looming, but I don't feel it.

I post content daily to social media, sharing what I've learned. I write blogs, do gallery events, and something I never thought I'd do again.

I have come full circle. I am teaching again. My own course. I have over thirty students. I wrote a book about it.

Of course I did!

COSMIC DREAMER
～ BETTY JAMPEL ～

HERE I AM, at sixty-four. I have been a daughter, a wife, a mother, a therapist and social worker, an ex-wife, lover, and now a matriarchal elder moving into my Crone years. Throughout these stages, I have been a student soaking up information, stories, and rich life experiences. I would say I have never been an expert in anything although I have certainly honed my skills, learned many hard life lessons, and collected many stories along the way.

I have been a social worker and therapist for most of my adult life. I have worked in hospitals, community agencies, universities, and schools. I've worked with children, adults, and elders in every stage of developmental life and psychiatric state, and now I work with people at the end stage of life and their families. I am also a psychedelic medicine facilitator for a clinical trial of psilocybin and doing Ketamine-assisted psychotherapy. Over the span of thirty-six years in the field, I've been trained and work with integrative and holistic modalities and consider myself a humanistic and transformational psychotherapist.

All this training and life experience has led to a profound interest in healing through working with non-ordinary states of consciousness. I have been delving and diving deeply, both personally and professionally, in these waters. And I would say that my life's work is now focused on using psychedelic medicines as an avenue to explore non-ordinary states of consciousness, and using those states to access wisdom, wellness, and guidance, for myself and others.

We in the West, are not accustomed to the language of Spirit and Nature. We are not encouraged or validated to "see" and acknowledge that which is not three dimensional and tangible to most. We tend to demonize, pathologize, and shun any reports/experiences of a non-ordinary nature. We are taught to believe that children have vivid imaginations, that dream states are imaginary, and that death is an end game. I am here to tell you that none of this is true, and this has become my passion: To educate and to create opportunities and a portal for transformational healing and growth, so that generations to come are open and enlightened, willing and able to access and express higher states of consciousness to make compassionate and life-sustaining choices.

We are taught to believe that children have vivid imaginations, that dream states are imaginary, and that death is an end game

I can say all these things, and everything I will write going forward, because I am no longer afraid. I stand in my truth unafraid of the judgments of others, no longer basing my self-worth on the opinions of others. It is that simple. And it has been quite freeing. Sometimes I wish I had learned this lesson earlier in my life, but no matter, this has been my path. Hard-won life lessons that this soul, on this earthly plane, at this time, in the family constellation and history it was born into, has led this beautiful being to its here and now. There is a magic and synchronicity and sacredness to life that I have come to accept.

Every day, I work with the terminally ill and dying and their family members. Everyone has had their own paths in life, which can influence how they leave their corporeal bodies behind and move into the spiritual realm. I have learned that we move into these realms simply because we are spiritual beings. Through my experiences and work with mediums, shamans, and spiritual practitioners, I've come to know this as a truth.

> *What death has to teach us is the meaning of life, and we have lost so much we need to regain.*

When I was a child, I often saw spirits and angels around me although I had no language to express it. As a baby in my crib in Brazil, I was sometimes left a little too long before someone attended to me. But I would quiet down when I was visited by beautiful angelic beings. As a young child, I would often see these ethereal folks hanging around the lobby of my apartment building. They didn't scare me, but I often wondered why they were there. I would fly up the stairs to my apartment, not so much to get away from them, but to return to my familiar reality. The one I knew everyone agreed on was "real" and what was "crazy". Many years later, I would recognize them as archangels as I began to connect with my spiritual abilities.

Many of these early experiences were tucked away deep inside of me. It wasn't until my pregnancies that I started to connect to something bigger than myself. I had challenging pregnancies. In the throes of early contractions, I did what most non-believers in the foxhole do. I prayed. It wasn't that I was a non-believer, but I wasn't connected to anything but my sentient body. I asked God or any other entities that looked over and took responsibility for good outcomes, to please save this as yet unborn child. I prayed very hard and stayed very still. For a very long time. I felt the sun come through the room, the warmth of the day around me. Suddenly, I felt a whoosh go through my body, from the top of my head down through my heart and lungs and into my swollen belly. I heard in my mind, "Everything is going to be all right. It's a girl." And it was.

With both pregnancies, I received this spiritual guidance and assistance, and with each child, I could feel a part of my own soul died and had gone into the children. They say having children is like wearing your heart on your sleeve, but it is also about giving over a part of yourself, and that's your spiritual essence. This essence is not tangible in the three-dimensional realm, but it is accessed when we are living outside the norms of conventional life and accessing non-ordinary states of being.

Being in the realm of dying, for the patient and those around them, is about accepting experiences that do not conform to conventional, three-dimensional reality. All sense of time loses its orientation during end-of-life days. Profound experiences occur. I have seen this magic happen in providing deathbed guidance.

But there is so much fear and unknown around end of life. Those who are dying can't or won't express what they are experiencing out of fear they will hurt those around them. Sadly, their loved ones don't get the chance to hear about some wondrous experiences. Just as we labor to come into this world in our own unique way, so do we labor to leave, and no two experiences are alike.

Anxiety and fear can often take hold at end of life. The Western world has taken this personal experience from the home and relegated dying and death to outside, impersonal cold institutions. This has shielded most generations of families from the intimate experience and knowledge of death. What death has to teach us is the meaning of life and we have lost so much we need to regain.

The continuity of life and death swing one into each other. Everybody dies, but no one is dead. This is a fundamental Buddhist and Eastern belief. People with near death experiences can tell you what had been said and done while they were technically dead because the essence of their soul is present and observing. A person near death can often tell you that a faraway sibling is dying or that a baby will be coming into the family. Such information is easily accessible because the soul is fluid, travelling between this plane and the next, observing and reporting all it sees. It is just a matter of those at the bedside believing it.

The sense of disconnection that people feel when their loved ones die, is often the core of their sadness and grief. Helping the grieving, especially those who experience long-term bereavement and unresolved grief, feel a sense of connection again to their loved one and their loved one's legacy, can offer comfort, solace, and relief. We can only do this work if we keep ourselves open to all possibilities of experiences.

> We are interconnected and this profound sense of unity is, I believe, what will inevitably save us. It is what has kept communities alive and thriving from earliest times.

We must allow ourselves to suspend our beliefs and to encompass things and realities we may never have thought possible. It is in this new dimension that we will find answers to big and small questions. When I hear that going into outer space is the next realm of adventure, I will disagree. Going within and seeing with ancient and Indigenous eyes, is what the world is yearning and moving towards.

We are moving into a new age of unity consciousness. We are a global community. It does not serve us to believe that what we do in one country or region of the world, doesn't affect someone else across the world. We are interconnected and this profound sense of unity is, I believe, what will inevitably save us. It is what has kept communities alive and thriving from earliest times. We need to reclaim our Indigenous roots to forge a new world order.

I have a deep belief that working with psychedelic medicines and plants is a way to move forward, as individuals and as a global society. I've had a deep interest in psychedelics since reading Carlos Castaneda as a college freshman. *Journey to Ixtlan: The Lessons of Don Juan*, encompasses the lessons that an anthropologist learned during his time studying with a Yaqui Indian shaman. Castaneda is at first a reluctant student, trying to rationalize the alternative realities he is experiencing. Through various experiences and some with the hallucinogenic plant, peyote, he finally comes to experience and accept that there are multi-dimensional realms of existence. These realms exist on parallel planes to what we experience on this earth plane. There is no past, present, and future, but rather a timeless and seamless existence of all sentient things on a continuum of endless time.

I grew up with Nancy Reagan's "Just Say No" war on drugs, famously depicted in a public service announcement "This Is Your Brain on Drugs", with an egg sizzling in a pan. I believed that drugs were generally "bad" and often saw the outcome of addiction in my mental health work. Many people still carry these messages and beliefs about these medicines. But the problem is that these messages were not accurate.

Plant medicines like peyote, ayahuasca, magic mushrooms, cannabis, tobacco, and other plants have been used for centuries by Indigenous peoples for healing and spiritual purposes. All of us are direct descendants, no matter our lineage, of these peoples and their practices. What these medicines do is connect us to the core unity of consciousness, and when we are in this state, we are pure love. We feel a connection to all life around us and to each other. In this state, we can make choices that uplift rather than hate and destroy.

The emergence once again of these medicines, and synthetic psychedelic medicines, which have the same profound impact, comes at another crossroads in history. The geopolitical, economic, and environmental crises we are now facing requires a deeper dive for solutions. As Einstein posited, we will not solve a problem with the same mind that created it. We are being called to reach deeper within ourselves to places that we ourselves are unfamiliar with. Even the Shadow Self, that part (or parts) of us we cannot let others see or even acknowledge. To be the light in this world, the solution rather than the problem, we must be willing to see what we bring to the table of humanity, which includes all the parts of ourselves. Doing this individually and then as a collective can start the road to a global understanding and to peaceful resolutions.

To be the light in this world, the solution rather than the problem, we must be willing to see what we bring to the table of humanity. All the parts of ourselves.

This has become my life's work: the use of legal psychedelic medicines in a safe and therapeutic setting to facilitate healing. It is a path driven by a passion to foster healing, justice, and peace. In the past, my younger self would balk at such audacity. *Who am I,* she would say, *to have such grand and grandiose goals?* But now that younger self is a glimmer behind me, and her voice, though sweet, has met her Elder, older, wiser self. It was easy to stay small in my life. Through transgenerational trauma and history, I learned that it was best to be inconspicuous. But through trauma-informed work, I am learning to move beyond those limitations.

The richness of a life well lived, creates a tapestry of experiences and wisdom that culminates in a fiercely held life. The Crone, in ancient and archetypal wisdom, symbolizes independence, confidence, and courage. She is a fully awakened and powerful woman, having insight, foresight, and inner sight. She brings forth her own wisdom as she is also a teacher and a leader in her community. She cares for the welfare of all beings. I carry this responsibility with great love in my heart as I do my work in this third and final chapter of my life. It is for me a gift I gladly return to my family, community, and all sentient beings for the privilege of this earthly life.

May it come to pass that peace, harmony, wellness, and sustainability can flourish into the next generations to come.

FINDING MEANING IN SOLITUDE AND COMMUNITY[1]

JEFF RASLEY

OUR NEPALI GUIDE, Ganesh, told us that the 14,000-foot summit of Pikey Peak was just a two-hour scramble up from our base camp at 10,000 feet. So, we'd summit the mountain and be back in base camp before dinnertime. Ganesh pointed out the trailhead just above the *goth* (yak herder's shelter) on the edge of our camp. We started up the trail with Ganesh leading, Mike in the rear, and me in between them.

After fifteen minutes hiking up the steep, rocky trail, Mike was struggling. I signaled that I was going on ahead. Fifteen minutes later, I looked back and saw Mike resting on a boulder. He was having trouble acclimatizing to the altitude. Ganesh and I waved to each other. The next time I looked down they were out of sight.

Clouds were rolling in, so I picked up the pace to reach the summit before the clouds would blot out the majestic Himalayan peaks I wanted to see. After another hour of hiking and scrambling

---

1 Adapted from a chapter in *You Have to Get Lost Before You Can Be Found*. See the Selected Bibliography for the full citation.

around boulders, I saw a series of stone steps cut into the side of the mountain. Beyond the last rock step was a rounded green hump. A bamboo arch with Buddhist prayer flags flapping in the wind was in the center of the summit.

I was surprised that the summit was grass-covered. I had expected a rocky top with a dusting of snow. But it was a comfy sort of summit, a pleasant place, not at all austere or forbidding. The view of the vast Himalayas from Kanchenjunga and Makalu in the east to the Everest Massif dead ahead and Annapurna in the distant west was awesome.

This was my first moment of complete solitude during the trek to Basa Village. The main purpose of the trek was to assist the village in the construction of a hydroelectric system to provide electricity to a remote area of Nepal that did not have any. The project was financed by a foundation of which Mike was chairman and I was president. Climbing Pikey Peak was to be a diversion from the work of our mission.

The moment of solitude passed too swiftly. After just a few minutes, clouds enveloped the summit. I could not see beyond the edge of the summit. I was inside the gray fog of a cloud. I assumed Mike and Ganesh had decided not to hike up to the summit and returned to camp.

The wind was picking up. It is unwise to be on an exposed summit, even a modest 14,000 foot one, during a storm. So, after a few minutes sitting in meditation, I hoisted my pack to head down.

I walked back to the edge of the green hump to begin my descent down the stone steps. But the stone steps had vanished. Visibility in the dense fog was down to about ten feet. The wind was picking up and slashing at me. I circled around the top of the mountain searching for the stone steps. I couldn't find them in the fog.

What the hell! I was fifty-seven years old in 2010, but fit and strong. It would be fun to break my own trail down the mountain.

I soon encountered a thick patch of scrub pine, but no trail. Since I wasn't sure which way to go around the stand of trees, I just bushwhacked straight on. It wasn't easy because the mountainside was steep.

I had to move from tree to tree, hanging on to branches or trunks, to keep from falling. The stand of trees ended above a rocky overhang. Without rope I couldn't down climb the rock face. I worked my way along the ledge and came to a frozen waterfall. Water was trickling under several inches of solid ice hugging a smooth ten-foot rock face.

I slid on my butt down the ten-foot ice chute and landed hard on my feet. But I kept my balance and wasn't hurt. Hurt and alone on the mountain would seriously detract from the enjoyment of this adventure.

I bushwhacked my way through the rhododendrons, hit another rocky outcropping, which I was able to climb down, and was then in a thicket of tea bushes. Every inch of ground was covered with tea plants and other ankle-grabbing vegetation. I could barely pull and push my feet through it. Progress was too slow. It was like walking in deep mud. I worked my way back to the rhododendron forest.

The detour forced me to veer off from the straight-line direction I thought would intersect the trail, but I was able to begin working my way downhill again. I grasped tree limbs for purchase to keep my balance as I struggled down the steep mountainside.

There was nothing to be worried about yet; more than two hours before sundown, and I still had plenty of energy. I had two granola bars in my pack for snacks. I didn't have any cold-weather clothes or a sleeping bag with me. The total up and down time from Pikey base camp to summit was supposed to be four hours. I was not prepared to be out after dark or to need food. But no worries yet, I was sure I'd be back in camp before sundown.

When I finally broke out of the rhododendron forest into a stand of tall spruce and pine trees, visibility was much better. I knew that the tall trees were just above the trail and hooray! There it was – the trail.

I turned left because I was sure that was the way to our campsite. I strode down the trail feeling bold and confident again. The anxiety that had started to creep into my mind evaporated. Getting lost for a little while and making my own trail down a mountain was just one more cool adventure in the Himalayas. I couldn't be too far from camp. I was getting a little hungry so I ate one of the granola bars. I saw boot and shoe prints on the dirt trail, so I was sure I was on the right track. We had not seen anyone else on the trail to base camp from Ngar Gompa (gompa is a Buddhist monastery and school), where we had camped the night before.

But something wasn't right. The trail kept descending. I clearly remembered that the trail from Ngar Gompa was a gradually ascending trail not a descending one. But I followed the trail another thirty minutes before I was absolutely convinced that I was going in the wrong direction. It made no sense. Who made the footprints I was following? But I must be going the wrong way. We had not gone down from Ngar, we had gone up!

I must have erred and should have gone right instead of left when I found the trail. I backtracked the half hour I'd spent walking left. I picked up the pace and ran a hundred yards or so every few minutes. It was getting late in the afternoon. Sundown would be at six o'clock. It was nearly five now. I needed to make time. I did not want to be out after dark. I had left both of my headlamps and my down jacket in my tent. Stupid! Hiking after dark without a headlamp and cold-weather clothes was not an attractive option. Anxiety crept back in.

I jogged past the woody area where I found the trail. The fog had cleared enough that I could see fifty yards or so. Twenty minutes later the trail ended abruptly. A rockslide had wiped out a hundred-yard stretch.

Could I pick my way across the rockslide? Traversing a mountainside across a rockslide without a rope or a partner would be very risky. If I fell and broke a bone or turned an ankle, I had no way to call for aid. I could see splotches of color through the fog on the side of the next mountain. It might be Ngar Gompa and shelter for the night. But to get there, I'd have to find a way across that dangerous rock field.

As the clouds moved out, I had another idea – maybe there was another trail. When I came down through the trees, it was possible I just couldn't see a trail that ascended instead of descended. No section of the trail we hiked from Ngar was wiped out by a landslide. There had to be another trail! Okay, so turn around again and go back. Look for a higher trail now that visibility had improved. I backtracked once again on the run.

I also started looking for caves and shelters just in case I had to spend the night on the mountainside.

Just past the point where I'd originally found the trail, I noticed a break in the trees. I stopped to check it out. Above the trail there was a little clearing in the woods I hadn't noticed on the descent. I found a broken-down fence and remains of some straw bales. It was a yak pasture. Yes! I remembered seeing it on the way to our campsite. Across the little pasture was another trail. And, there was a Buddhi arrow!

Buddhi drew an arrow to mark the direction to take at every trail intersection on the trek to Bassa. This was a Buddhi arrow showing me the way.

Dusk was rapidly approaching. I alternated jogging and speed walking every couple hundred yards. I soon came to another trail intersection. I was sure I should take the upward trail, so without hesitation I turned to the left heading uphill. Another twenty minutes and I was back at the pasture where I'd started. Argh! Somehow, I had run and walked in a circle! I wanted to gnash my teeth and tear my hair.

Instead, I stopped and ate a granola bar. I needed to regain composure. Throughout the afternoon, I'd chanted the Buddhist mantra: *Om mani padme hum*. But I was lost and needed to be found. I began to sing:

>Amazing Grace, how sweet the sound,
>That saved a wretch like me.
>I once was lost but now am found,
>Was blind, but now I see.
>T'was Grace that taught my heart to fear.
>And Grace, my fears relieved.
>How precious did that Grace appear
>The hour I first believed.
>Through many dangers, toils and snares

I have already come;
'Tis Grace that brought me safe thus far
and Grace will lead me home.

I was calm again and strode back down the circular trail at a steady pace. This time, I went straight in the direction Buddhi's arrow pointed. The sun had sunk behind a mountain to the west. But even in the gathering dusk I now saw familiar boot prints. I recognized Hamid's unique print made by the shoes I'd given him from Changing Footprints, one of the NGOs supporting our foundation's development projects in Basa.

I had lost sight of Ganesh and Mike five hours ago. Now that I was confident I was on the correct route back to our camp, the feeling of joyful pleasure in my little solitary adventure returned. I was lost but now I was found.

Night had settled on the mountain by the time I sighted lights at our campsite. I knew Ganesh and the crew would be worried and upset, so I began yelling as I approached the camp. No one responded. I didn't see anyone. I poked my head into Mike's tent. He was asleep. Ram came out of the goth he was using for a kitchen. He said that Ganesh, Buddhi, Nirman, and Hamid were all up on the mountain looking for me.

Damn! Well, what did I expect? Of course, they'd be looking for me.

Ratanbir came with me. We yelled and hollered as we jogged up the rocky path toward the summit of Pikey Peak. About fifteen minutes up, we saw Ganesh waving down at us. Then we saw Buddhi higher up acknowledging Ganesh's signaling whistle.

When we were all back down and gathered in the meal tent, we learned that poor Hamid had hiked all the way to the top but had found no sign of me. Oh well, everyone was in a good mood and happy that I was back in the bosom of our little community.

It felt very good to share the warmth of our meal tent with the guys, to laugh about my execrable sense of direction, to pass around plates of *dal bhat*, cups of hot tea, and finish off the meal with a shared bottle of *rakshi* (local spirits).

Being alone and lost on the mountain made me feel very small and vulnerable. The congenial fellowship in the meal tent reminded me that we humans are social beings. Community is an essential aspect of our humanity.

> *We humans are social beings. Community is an essential aspect of our humanity.*

I enjoy many solitary activities, like reading, solo kayaking, meditating, and writing. It feels good to be isolated in those experiences. But being part of a family and participating actively in communities I care about really makes life meaningful.

One wisdom I have gained is that to be healthy we need a balance of alone time and together time. Too much time in isolation and we may become insensitive and self-centered. Too much time in the company of others will leave us craving to get away, so that we can pay attention to our own needs. One of life's pleasures is sharing memories of cool experiences with others and hearing about equally meaningful experiences from them. How meaningful are experiences, if you do not have family and friends who are either with you or you can tell them about it?

A LIFETIME OF RESILIENCE, RENEWAL, AND REINVENTION

～ ALAN STEIN ～

I WAS BORN THE youngest of three children, with an older sister and brother. Our father was one of six children, of whom only his sister and he survived past the age of ten. He caught polio when he was six years old and grew up as a disabled boy with pencil thin legs. He eventually needed braces on both legs to help support his weight so he could walk, albeit with difficulty and a serious limp. His parents, having lost their other four children to a variety of causes, were angry that he was an ill child and had very little empathy for him.

Our mother was an only child who grew up in a very poor but loving family. She married one of the few men available during WWII and was totally unprepared for the emotional abuse and indentured life she had to endure. But, having no safety network, she stayed in spite of the abuse and financial hardships. However, through it all, she maintained a sense of humor and did the best she could do to raise her three latchkey kids, since she always had to work and was never home.

Our father lived a frustrating life, wanting to be a doctor, but reliant on his parents, who did not support his aspirations, and instead took advantage of his financial dependence on them. They demanded that he work for them 24/7 managing their real estate properties. Although intelligent, with many ideas, his parents were self-serving, narcissistic, and angry at him for being a sick boy. He was always a "disappointment" since he could not do everything that they demanded.

> We had no family or support network that we could rely on since our home was one of irrational and conditional love.

Our father had no time to raise children and expressed, on many occasions, that we would have to fend for ourselves. My sister, brother, and I grew up in a home with constant verbal and physical threats, humiliations, and spankings until our father got what he wanted from us. Our mother would console us but express that she was fearful of our father and powerless to protect us. Our whole extended family knew our father was a frustrated, temperamental hothead and therefore had little to do with us so as not to become a focus of his anger. As children we were commanded and had no choice but to obey – to be seen but not heard.

Our mother and father mastered the art of hearing but not *listening* – discussions were in fact lectures in disguise. Any point of disagreement was debated until we each relented or succumbed to the threat of or actual spankings, homelessness, no inheritance, etc., unless we did what was demanded.

In the end, we each realized we had no family or support network that we could rely on since our home was one of irrational and conditional love. As we grew up, we each would have to develop the skills, intuition, foresight, enlightenment, and resilience to survive as adults.

As I have grown and matured, I've learned to credit and respect our father for his resilience, displayed by his physical and financial resolve to meet the business and physical challenges in his life to survive, prosper, and take care of his family. While he can never be forgiven for his brutal emotional torment and myopic approach to those around him, enlightenment has provided me with a greater understanding of the difficulties he had to face to overcome his physical impairments, emotional torment, and financial gyrations from his parents.

Ironically, I subsequently had to face my own physical challenges over and over again during my life. To meet my mental, physical, and financial challenges of survival, I had to constantly adapt and hyper focus, avoid distraction, depression, gloom and doom, and make whatever sacrifice was necessary to support my family and build my business.

While a junior in college, at the age of twenty, I bumped a mole on the shin of my right leg. It was the only large mole on my body, about half the diameter of a dime, and it bled. As it healed, it developed an odd-looking red ring around the black center. Upon researching moles with red rings, I discovered that a mole with that description could be cancerous. Following excision by a dermatologist it was determined to have become a melanoma . . . and my unique journey began . . .

I graduated college with a BBA degree and, with limited opportunities in South Florida, got a job with a local insurance company in 1973. I immediately began to pursue my MBA degree in night school and would spend the next four years earning my graduate degree. While attending night school I got married and, four years later, at age twenty-six, felt a lump in my right groin and found out that the melanoma had metastasized to multiple lymph nodes in that leg. Subsequently, I underwent an extensive volume of X-rays and diagnostic routines. When I inquired about the overuse of the X-ray machine, and its potential for causing health problems later in life, I was told the doctors were not worried about future issues they just wanted to 'save' me in that moment. I was ultimately told I had a fifteen percent chance of surviving the next five years.

To keep my health problems confidential, I took some vacation time for my surgery. When I returned to work, I explained my difficulty walking as having fallen off the roof onto a sprinkler head and that I would subsequently need time to heal but that I could keep working.

I worked for that insurance company, in multiple positions, always hoping to get into sales since that was where the higher salaries were earned. However, when I finally got promoted into a sales position (1979), I was twenty-eight and the U.S. economy was entering a recession, interest rates were rising to twenty percent, and I knew that I could never meet my quota requirements.

Undaunted, I spent six months traveling all over the country randomly cold calling any retail outlet that I thought might have a business that could survive extremely high interest rates. Six months into my search, I discovered an undeveloped insurance market opportunity. Fortunately, I had the knowledge and experience to develop that idea within the company and, a year and a half later, submitted everything I had developed to the governing insurance company committee for approval to distribute and sell a new product into a new market.

At first, the company said okay but then management wanted to hold off putting resources towards an unproven product in the middle of a recession. With all the work done and the product ready to go, I eventually chose to resign from the company in 1982 conditioned on the fact that I would be the exclusive agent for the company and would assume all of the risk for distribution, sales, and claim losses for this new product. Since I was only thirty-three, and five years post-cancer surgery, had little to no assets, and very little to lose, I said okay.

However, within twelve months of leaving the company (1983), I experienced a sharp random pain behind my left knee. The diagnosis was another melanoma metastasis, which required immediate excision. Then, post-surgery, the full diagnostic results were disclosed to me: the doctors advised that they had also discovered a new and different kind of cancerous growth on my right lung, which required the removal of my entire right lung before the end of that same year. As you can imagine, no one thought I would survive much longer due to the metastatic melanoma plus lung cancer.

Since I now had a wife and young son, I repeated my prior pattern and hyper focused on my business, to make sure that my family would be okay. It distracted me from my fear of dying since it gave me purpose.

Every morning, I could recognize my palpable fear but was able to redirect my energy to deal with my growing business needs one day at a time.

Unfortunately, over time, the health, financial issues, and business demands took a toll on my marriage and after twenty years of initial bliss and hell later (my wife was waiting for me to die and had lost that loving feeling because she felt trapped and, with unrealized expectations, was very unhappy), I decided to get divorced in 1995.

During the next five years, while single and undistracted, and not having to deal with any other health challenges, my business and personal life thrived.

Five years after divorcing my first wife, I met the woman who would become my second wife. But then, after feeling confident subsequent to sixteen continuously healthy years, during our courtship and still in my forties, I developed a serious aggressive case of prostate cancer and had to have my prostate removed in 2000.

We married and lived happily for the majority of our twenty-two-year marriage. We found happiness in spite of the fact that shortly after getting married and healing from the prostate surgery, the muscle cut to get to the prostate did not heal properly and developed another type of cancerous tumor in 2003 (Desmoid tumor). This required the removal of my right rectus muscle and installation of an abdominal mesh net.

Since the rectus muscle holds back the intestines, I required the installation of a mesh net for abdominal support to avoid a blowout hernia. Consistent with this latest streak of bad luck, the mesh was compromised, and I had to deal with an infection that turned into sepsis and required the removal of the mesh, debridement of the infection, and reinstallation of a replacement mesh in 2004. Thankfully, I had wonderful doctors and a terrific supportive wife who stepped up to help me get through this very challenging period.

Post my 2004 surgery, my business was still growing and life was good, my marriage was great and my follow-up medical tests continued to be unremarkable for almost two years. Then, in 2006, during a routine PET Scan, my left hip lit up and ultimately revealed another

My Gift of Life

1972 - Melanoma right shin – skin graft from right thigh to right shin.

1978 - Melanoma metastasis right groin – removed 22 lymph nodes from right groin of which three were malignant.

1983 - Melanoma metastasis left medial calf – wide excision of calf muscle tissue from left popliteal.

1983 - Mucoepidermoid carcinoma of the right lung – right lung removed.

2000 - Prostate cancer - prostate removed.

2003 - Abdominal Fibromatosis (Desmoid) – removed right rectus muscle and installed abdominal mesh.

2003 - Mycobacterial infection – M. Fortuitum – removed mesh, debridement of infected tissue and over nine months of antibiotics.

2004 - Reinstallation of mesh – Mesh failure resulted in large abdominal hernia on right side of the abdomen.

2006 - Leiomyosarcoma left hip – removed cancerous tissue in left hip with Brachytherapy spot radiation treatment immediately thereafter.

virulent cancer, Leiomyosarcoma (my fifth type of cancer), which required surgery and local radiation and had a very poor prognosis for the five years after the surgery.[2]

Once again, the ability to hyper focus on my business helped me compartmentalize the trauma of my fifth different type of cancer and eighth surgery. As a result of my constant health challenges, my second wife began to study holistic alternatives, became a health coach (www.gohealthywithkaren.com), changed my diet, found health professionals with alternative modalities to combine with traditional medicine and recommended supplements to fight inflammation, cancer, cholesterol, boost my immune system and more. Through her efforts and guidance, I've not experienced another cancer or serious health incident since 2006. Over the next seventeen years, she and I evolved from lovers and best friends to best friends because our

---

[2] In my opinion, all but my initial cancer and lung cancer were in my abdominal area and believe those cancers resulted from overuse of X-ray equipment in 1978. X-ray dosage and targeting have been significantly improved using today's guidelines.

careers, age difference, and constant family drama put us on separate paths to happiness. So, after twenty-two years of marriage, we divorced (2023), continue to be best friends, and are fully supportive of each other.

Now entering the third chapter of life, I'm happy, live in a state of gratitude and purpose, with my scars of survival but without chronic pain, and am excited and energized to make the most of the time I have left. I feel healthy and strong, am driven to socialize and connect to a whole new network of professional and social contacts and create brand new businesses with new young partners who can carry on when I'm gone.

During the latter part of 2023, I started two new companies and am now networking all over the Tri-County region where I live. I've made over five hundred new contacts and attended over twenty-five networking events in the last six months, recently signed my first new client, and am excited to grow my new businesses in 2024 and beyond.

Although this is the third phase of life, it's my umpteenth time to start again! Having a daily objective with purpose, and a focus on business and social activities that are mentally stimulating, surrounded by a professional and social network of intelligent vibrant individuals seeking knowledge and enlightenment, I have no time to feel old and tired, nonproductive and without purpose – that's not my chosen path.

In spite of, and while enduring the multitude of health challenges through the chronology of surgeries and cancers listed (see box) I was a founder of a religious institution and a city commissioner. I kept my health issues confidential so those narrow-minded individuals in power would not think to stop my progress because they might speculate that I'd get sick on the job.

I live my life with gratitude, purpose, positivity and joy, constantly seeking to learn new things, to stay mentally active and live responsibly because I know how lucky I am. I don't have the time, inclination, or desire to be a victim and refuse to dwell in the past or make excuses for why I didn't make other choices.

Life is a gift to be enjoyed as best as your individual circumstances allow. I will always live with the knowledge that it can be taken away at any moment!

In the end, I hope to provide a legacy for those I love and the charities I support (cancer.org and handyinc.org) and to fulfill the purpose for which I survived.

FROM PERSONAL TRAGEDY TO PUBLIC TRIUMPH: THE CREATION OF "GRIEF 2 GROWTH"

∽ BRIAN SMITH ∾

AS I STAND at retirement's doorstep, I can't help but reflect on the wisdom of Kierkegaard, who once said, "Life can only be understood backwards, but must be lived forwards." It's funny how, as we accumulate more life experiences and candles on our birthday cake, the puzzle pieces of our existence start falling into place. Some might say it all finally makes sense just when we're nearing the finish line, as if that wisdom is lost when we cross the line. But I know better; I see the death of my physical body as the start of a thrilling new chapter in a never-ending story.

At the 'advanced age' of sixty-two, I've held down eight professional gigs since my high school days, navigating through four distinct careers. I've danced with divorce, been shown the door by employers twice, and had my heart shattered by the loss of my beloved daughter, Shayna. Back then, none of these trials made any sense to me. But as Kierkegaard predicted, life's river of time keeps flowing, and with it comes a deeper understanding. I've discovered that the most profound meaning often emerges from the most challenging chapters of my life. I didn't just endure these adversities; they sculpted me into who I am today. Without them, I would be less.

My early years unfolded in the heart of Columbus, Ohio, within a devoutly religious family. I was born into the expectation of being a devout Christian, with my grandfather as the pastor of our church. I was introduced to a God who seemed angry and judgmental, viewing me as an enemy due to my 'original sin.' Baptism, speaking in tongues, and receiving the 'Holy Ghost' became things I needed to do to be 'saved.' So, I did them. Yet, I never felt comfortable with the God of my youth.

And then there was the burden of racial prejudice during the tumultuous 1960s. I struggled to comprehend why people despised me purely based on my skin color. In my eyes, my mother and brother, who were lighter skinned, seemed 'white', leaving me pondering, "Why am I Black?" I didn't understand race.

Around age seven, my maternal grandfather, a deeply religious man, passed away in the most dramatic fashion possible – in church while giving his 'testimony.' I was left baffled. Why didn't God protect him? How could he vanish in the blink of an eye while doing God's work? This experience and the doctrine of heaven and hell sowed the seeds of my profound fear of death. This fear clung to me for decades, causing panic attacks well into my thirties and forties.

In my early twenties, I confronted my racial identity, accepting the reality that the world would always see me as Black despite my yearning to be simply 'Brian.' My mid-twenties ushered in a phase of intense spiritual exploration. I embarked on a quest to decipher the enigma of religion. They told me God loved me unconditionally and that He was a benevolent Creator. Yet, they also preached damnation for merely being the creation He made me to be. My journey through this spiritual maze led me to devour books on religion, philosophy, science, and the afterlife.

My educational background was in Chemical Engineering, and I embarked on a professional journey as an Operations Engineer for a gas utility company. However, the allure of sales quickly beckoned, promising more financial rewards. So, I ventured into the marketing world, landing a role at none other than IBM, the mecca of tech. Eight years later, I found myself in various sales positions within the computer industry. Little did I know that this experience would lay the foundation for my future endeavors, including my foray into online retail, where I crafted websites and branding for our product lines. These skills later proved invaluable as I ventured into life coaching and podcasting. I may not be a one-man show anymore, but I still roll up my sleeves for a significant part of my production work.

The middle years of my life weren't without their share of trials. I weathered two job terminations and faced the turbulence of a traumatic divorce in my mid-twenties. However, those tumultuous years left me with invaluable lessons that continue to resonate nearly four decades later. I remember my wife Tywana wishing I weren't a divorcé. But, as I told her, even those years ago, that was a necessary and beneficial part of my journey.

I contemplated legal action when Sun Microsystems handed me the pink slip for no justifiable reason. Instead, I embraced my fate and believed it would lead to something better. And it did, as I stepped into the most financially rewarding role of my career. The second job termination prompted me to launch my online retail business, a venture I have nurtured for twenty-one years.

Then came the heart-wrenching blow. On June 24th, 2015, my 15-year-old daughter, Shayna Elayne Smith, peacefully transitioned from this world to the next in her sleep. At that time, I was running my online retail empire, and Shayna had just completed her first year of high school, only her second year in a public school after being homeschooled for her early years. Kayla, my other daughter, had just finished her first year of college, and Tywana worked with me on the business.

No words can describe the depth of despair I felt after Shayna's departure. "Devastated" barely scratches the surface. It took three long years to regain some semblance of balance. Joining *Helping Par-*

ents Heal was a turning point. As a Caring Listener, I reached out to countless parents who had also suffered the indescribable loss of a child. I led online meetings and interviewed individuals for our sessions. Then, an intuitive friend and medium suggested I take a life coaching course she had stumbled upon. I wasn't seeking another career shift; I was in my late fifties, and my hair care business was chugging along. Retirement was rapidly approaching. But, I heeded her advice and took the course, trusting her intuition as much as I trusted mine. Ironically, she didn't take the course.

I hired a business coach to help me with my retail business. That's when it struck me that everything I had endured since Shayna's passing had paved the way for this transformation. The coach wasn't for my existing business. The coach was to help me launch something new.

A week after Shayna's departure, I started a blog, initially intended as a personal journal of my grief journey, in case Kayla or other family members found it interesting. While *Helping Parents Heal* was instrumental in my healing process, at *Helping Parents Heal*, I also acquired the skills to help others and honed my interview and presentation skills over the years. My retail business web development expertise proved invaluable for creating my coaching website. It was a career shift decades in the making.

I channeled all that newfound knowledge into my book, *Grief 2 Growth: Planted. Not Buried.* I revamped my website, delved into the world of podcasting, and recorded my initial YouTube videos. Today, I sit here with nearly three hundred podcast episodes under my belt, a best-selling book, and the honor of being a distinguished speaker and workshop presenter at the IANDS conference.

IANDS – the International Association for Near Death Studies – stands at the forefront of research into near-death experiences. When I think about the power of manifestation, I'm often in awe of my ability to bring forth change. At conferences, people approach me, expressing how profoundly my work has touched their lives. My daily work is working with people in grief, giving them a new lease on life.

I spend my evenings speaking via Zoom to various groups. As one friend said, "Changing lives, one Zoom at a time."

Meanwhile, my daughter Kayla embarked on her career path in mental health counseling after Shayna's passing, completing her undergraduate and master's degrees to work as a behaviorist. Tywana threw herself into *Helping Parents Heal*, offering solace and support to parents who have experienced the unimaginable loss of a child. Together, we forge ahead, Shayna guiding us from the other side.

> Death no longer signifies the end to me; it's a transition, like a child evolving into an adult or graduating from high school.

The deeper I delve into what we typically refer to as 'the afterlife', it becomes evident that it's merely the next chapter in the grand book of existence. The more I learn, the more I realize how much I'll never know. I'm committed to pursuing knowledge for as long as I draw breath. Death no longer signifies the end to me; it's a transition, like a child evolving into an adult or graduating from high school.

As I tinker with my website, refining my courses and one-on-one offerings for clients, I think about the books I'd like to pen in the coming year. There's still much work that lies ahead of me. I've got a legacy to wrap up before I move on to where Shayna is, and our shared work continues on the other side of the veil.

EMBRACING LIFE'S TAPESTRY WITH ANIMALS

~ TAMI HENDRIX ~

THIS IS A story about friends on a journey – moments strung together forming a life tapestry. Story moments are like the individual stitches that join together to reveal a shimmering work of art – one that can only be truly seen and appreciated when the story is complete. Ultimately, it is a story about us all and how transformation comes whether we are ready or not.

From the time I was a kid, animals were my very best friends. They spoke a language I could understand; they spoke from their heart and soul. This always made perfect sense to me, so there was never any breakdown in communication like I observed between people, especially adults. With animals, I could be myself. I could be a fun-loving child, rather than the adult in a child's body that was my family role. The animals showed me my own secret garden filled with magic, mystery, and a sense of belonging in a world that often made no sense.

It didn't surprise me as I grew into adulthood that this tendency to connect with animals would follow me everywhere. Apparently, animals were an integral part of my life's path.

In April 2004, a surprise package came – a sweet, fluffy white Lab puppy who needed rescuing. A random photo of puppies at a local shelter captured my attention, propelling me straight to him. He was with his siblings – all cute, fluffy, and adorable. All needing homes. When I cradled him in my arms and he looked into my eyes, he felt familiar, as if we already knew each other. And even though I felt an immediate and deep connection, I did not take him home. It just didn't make sense. Two days later, I received a call from a friend asking me if I was going to adopt him. That call saved Murphy's life: the day after I picked him up, a terrible virus swept through the shelter, and all his siblings perished. Looking back, I wish I had taken them all.

Murphy brought joy and loving kindness and the most huggable neck ever. We were instant soulmates. Like a mother with a new baby, I delighted in each of his milestones, taking hundreds of puppy photos, including a photo of him holding a tulip in his mouth like a dashing gentleman. He had a silky kindness and gentle soul presence that earned him the title: Dalai Lama of All Dogs. I couldn't have felt happier or more complete.

Then, in December 2004, my life changed forever.

My sister passed in a tragic car accident. I wasn't prepared for her to pass, though she had lived a tumultuous life, and I had often thought she wouldn't live long. In my mind, I had already experienced enough big losses to last a lifetime and had decided I was done with grief. I was angry. Thoughts bubbled up like a spewing volcano:

How dare she just up and leave me to deal with this?

She didn't even tell me ahead of time!

No one gave me the memo!

She didn't ask me how I would feel!

The reality was that I didn't want to feel. Period. And this was forcing me to do just that. Now, I know these thoughts were not rational or logical, or even terribly kind. In her defense, she obviously didn't owe me any notice ahead of time. And when I looked back, she had given me a "head's up" two weeks before in a casual phone call where we were just catching up. But I had worked hard at creating a life with few disturbances. I had long ago decided: no more upheavals for me.

Wrong.

I know now that transformation occurs at the edge of our comfort zones. And mine had just been blown wide open. Transformation is a cracking open of all defenses and heart barricades, all "this is the way life is supposed to be," to reveal bits and pieces of our soul, the fractured parts we've kept locked away.

> *Transformation is a cracking open of all defenses and heart barricades, all "this is the way life is supposed to be," to reveal bits and pieces of our soul, the fractured parts we've kept locked away.*

Her leaving marked the beginning of my descent into the pits of grief and sadness, as every prior loss (my father's suicide, my mother's excommunication of me and death, and all the traumatic experiences I had lived) came to pay me a visit. Grief came up like a swamp Gollum, torturing my thoughts and mind and, worst of all, my heart. Life became gray. I went numb.

I resorted to what I had always done as a child: I sought out the animals. Murphy was always by my side, which gave me great comfort. I hugged him. A lot.

But every night, I would sneak off from the family to sit with Snoopy, a patient, kind, and loving Hound mix who was like a mother to us all. And since I was a motherless daughter, she was the perfect match. Snoopy had her own transformation by going blind, but she seemed to be able to handle this change with a grace and acceptance I had always admired.

No one in my family knew the depths of my despair. During the day, I would function as if nothing had occurred. I was a mom and a business owner and had a busy life with the kids and animals. Life had gone on. Yet, every night, I would disappear to tuck her in. She and I would hunker down, soft music playing in the background, while I hugged her neck sobbing and rocking back and forth.

I felt orphaned. Again.

This went on for months. I didn't realize it at the time, but the very support I needed – a friend, a comforting mother or sister – came in the form of animals. Healing hurts.

Apparently, this was a group effort in the animal kingdom. Murphy, Snoopy, and then … Katie.

The day I found Katie was like any other day since my sister had passed; I was going through the motions of living. On a hot September day, I was returning from picking up my son from school when my eye caught movement in the bushes. I slowed down enough to see a tiny nose poking through the leaves and twigs. Something didn't feel right. Sure enough, it was a puppy – one that needed help. The classic 'puppy abandoned on the side of the road' ploy. I pulled over.

I went up to her slowly and said softly, "I'm here to help. You don't have to be afraid." I sat down. She studied me suspiciously, peeking through the openings in the brush. Then she disappeared out of sight, back into the swampy grass.

Apparently, she needed a moment to think.

I wasn't sure if she had left by way of the swampy jungle, or if she was still there. Suddenly I heard a crunching noise, and out popped this tiny puppy no more than three months old. Scrapes and cuts covered her nose and face, and she had big patches of fur missing all over her body. We stared at each other, not sure what to do next.

I stood very slowly and made my way to her. When I got close enough to touch her, I stopped and asked, "Are you okay with me picking you up?"

That was my first lesson with Katie – always ask permission. She took a tentative step toward me, so I reached down to pick her up. Her little body burned with heat; it was so red and inflamed. When I scooped her up, she immediately laid her head against my shoulder. I wanted to cry. My heart felt such an overwhelming rush of pure love – something I hadn't felt in quite some time. Healing had begun in earnest. I could feel my joy returning and my heart smiling.

Many animals would come over the years, often in very magical and mysterious ways, through dreams, photos, coincidences. I would know intuitively they were meant to stay. They came to heal and to follow their own soul paths, just like humans do. They came to live long lives, make friends, know what family means, and live to their highest potential.

While my family of origin provided the training ground to hone my intuitive skills, develop compassion, and see from the soul's perspective, the animals taught me about life, death, and what matters most. Through their unconditional love, willingness to forgive humans, and their readiness to heal from even the most horrific experiences, I learned how to transform challenges into opportunities and grief into peace.

Katie and the animals have always said, "It is not what gifts we have; it's what we do with those gifts that matters." And just like stories, our gifts are meant to be shared.

What gifts have you gleaned from your life? Take a look at your experiences, good or bad, amazing or tragic, and I'll guarantee there's a story to be told, a lesson to be learned, a gift to be shared.

Our stories are chapters that form the tapestry of our lives. For both animals and humans, once they are shared, they become the portal for healing and the gateway to true transformation.

My childhood experiences forged a deep connection to my spirit and soul, and the animals showed me my life's path as a healer, animal intuitive, and compassionate medium. Through a process I call Soul-Speak, an organic, intuitive conversation originating on a heart and soul level, I help connect pets with their humans to heal deep soul wounds and broken hearts.

JOURNEY BEYOND: EXPLORING THE MYSTERIES OF LIFE, DEATH, AND CREATION

◈ JULIE RYAN ◈

We Are Creative Beings

THROUGHOUT OUR LIVES, we are imbued with an innate creativity that shapes our existence. From the very moment we incarnate, we embark on a journey of creation. We build families, homes, relationships, careers, and even our personal styles. Our creative essence is in constant motion, guiding us to shape our world as we see fit. But what about the creation that happens when we leave this earthly realm?

> *In the grand tapestry of existence, our journey doesn't end with death, it merely takes on a new form.*

In the grand tapestry of existence, our journey doesn't end with death, it merely takes on a new form. Just because someone reaches a certain age doesn't signify the cessation of their creativity. Instead, it signifies a transition into something new and different, customized to the unique stage of life they find themselves in.

Creativity Knows No Age

Age is not a barrier to creativity. Consider iconic celebrities like Cher, Jane Fonda, Steven Tyler, the Rolling Stones, and Sir Paul McCartney. Each one of these people continue to thrive creatively well into their 70s, 80s, and moving towards their 90s. Their enduring careers serve as a testament to the boundless nature of human creativity.

Even death is not the end – it is a transition. We all have a hand in creating our own passage from this world to the next. Each of us determines where, when, how, and with whom we depart. The circumstances surrounding our final moments are completely a product of our own creation.

In addition, our journey doesn't begin at birth, it starts long before that. Just like in death, our spirit has complete control over where and when we are born and to whom we are born, so our lives have a trajectory allowing our spirit to explore and experience whatever it wishes.

Unfolding Experiences

Life is a series of unfolding experiences, each leading to new adventures. Take me, for example. As a serial entrepreneur (founded nine companies in five industries), and inventor of surgical devices sold throughout the world, I never envisioned my mid-sixties would lead me to a career focusing on spirituality and personal growth.

However, a simple phone call can change the course of our lives forever. When I received a life-altering call informing me of my mother's unexpected transition into hospice care, it shaped the trajectory of my life, career, and spiritual journey.

After a nearly 600-mile overnight drive to be with my mother, I witnessed many miraculous occurrences during her last day. Most importantly, I discovered the profound connection between the physical and spiritual planes. My psychic medium and intuitive abilities, learned ten years previously, helped my mother and me navigate the spiritual aspects of the dying process and taught me invaluable insights to share with dying individuals and their families worldwide. I witnessed angelic and spirit presences during my mother's transition, experiences that helped reshape my understanding of life, death, and beyond.

Prodding from a Dead Pope

Sometimes, we receive guidance from unexpected sources. That's what happened to me when the spirit of a dead pope appeared during meditation. Pope Clement VI told me my life's mission was to educate people throughout the world about the dying process, which has been distorted by cultures and religions. His message was clear: people need to know the truth about the beauty of one's passing and how they're surrounded by angels and spirits of deceased loved ones and pets.

Sharing Insights

In my book *Angelic Attendants: What Really Happens As We Transition From This Life Into The Next* (available for free at www.julieryangift.com), I describe the final hours leading up to my mother's passing. I explore the spiritual transformations and rituals that unfolded as my family gathered to say their farewells. My psychic medium insights offer a unique lens through which to understand the profound transition from this world to the next, an experience we will all share with the passing of a loved one and eventually, when we ourselves transition from this life into the next.

A Mother's Final Gift

It wasn't until much later, after my initial grieving period, that I realized the profound gift my mother had given me and through me, the people of the world. I developed a deeper understanding of the spiritual

> *We all are creative beings, constantly evolving and shaping our experiences.*

dimensions of life and death, knowledge that ancient peoples have known since the beginning of time, reflected in the prayers and rituals of various cultures, religions and belief systems. These insights aligned perfectly with the psychic experiences I had during my mother's final hours.

Embracing Life's Mysteries

The simple truth is, we all are creative beings, constantly evolving and shaping our experiences. Life's journey and the journey beyond are extensions of this creative expression, inviting us to embrace the mysteries of life, death, and creation with open hearts and minds. Most importantly, remember to enjoy every moment of your incredible journey!

PART 3

LIVING YOUR BEST LIFE

"Excitement doesn't knock at your door any less when you're older than when you're younger. It's just that when you're younger, You're more likely to open the door and let it in."

—Marianne Wilson

"Sometimes you have to give a little push, one way or the other, to get past the depression, low self-esteem, unhealthy relationships, procrastination, or whatever is holding you back from living your best life."

—Mary Morrison

A MOTHER'S LOVE AND THE PROMISE
⁜ FAUST RUGGIERO ⁜

THERE MAY BE no force in the human experience more potent than the love of a mother for her children. It is a warm world of brilliant light that wraps itself around everything and everyone it touches.

I experienced that love as a young boy and throughout my thirty-five years with our mother. An exceptionally intelligent person, she was an executive secretary, and for five years, was an administrative assistant at the Pentagon. She was insightful, and always compassionate. She was a strong woman, and when our father suffered a serious stroke at the age of forty-two, she, without complaints, went back to work, while raising their four children.

> *All too often, the lessons we learn from those who are significant in our lives are not understood until those people are taken from us.*

In the summer of 1984, she was diagnosed with liver cancer. The surgeons felt that they had removed the entire tumor. However, the cancer resurfaced a few years later, and in the fall of 1989, she passed with all four children by her bedside.

All too often, the lessons we learn from those who are significant in our lives are not understood until those people are taken from us. Ours was never a family that expressed much outward emotion, though the love, commitment, and dedication to each other was always there. My mother and I enjoyed a special bond. Though she was trained in the business world, she could have easily been the counselor I became. My father was a loving man, but not emotionally expressive, so our family was loving, but not demonstrative.

As my mother was coming to the last year of her life, I thought that the best gift I could give her was to become that person who would be demonstratively loving, not only on an emotional level, but also on a verbal one. So, in the summer of 1988, as I opened my private practice, I made a commitment to myself that her legacy would live through me, and that I would become that loving person who is willing to extend myself beyond my own perceived limitations and wrap the love she taught me around myself and everyone and everything I touched.

In this life, it is often the ashes that give way to an internal renaissance, to the rebirth of a person that creates a new life path, possessing the potential to change the world. It didn't take me long to realize that while my mother was still alive, I was still living through her. By that I mean I was following her lead, but never really establishing my own. I think, very often, it's the void that instigates the creation of that new life path. My mother's death created that new life path for me. Someone who loves unconditionally as my mother did not only leads by example, they also have a tendency to instill love on a deep spiritual level, which is not realized until it's called upon to be put in motion.

My mother's life and eventually her passing forced me to look deep inside myself. Sometimes, without understanding it, we tend to allow significant people to not only define who we are, but to help us as we express ourselves. Then, all of a sudden, that service is unavailable to us, we must pick up the pieces and define who we are. I was fortunate enough to have much of the information I needed if I was willing to understand my mother's life and its impact on me, but to move forward and embrace my world as my own person.

Making the choice to become vulnerable can be challenging, but it also opens the door to allow those parts of ourselves that we have protected for so long to become an active part of who we are. I have always been a very private person. At the same time, I always knew that the Lord gave me gifts for a reason, and that it was time for me to unleash those gifts on the world.

One of the most important self-realizations I had at this time was the understanding that defining myself as a private person was also causing me to set boundaries, and those boundaries interfered in the expression of my own personal gifts. My ability to understand other people, to help them define the inner light in their own lives was being seriously affected by my decision to remain a private person.

There's nothing wrong with being private. The concern for me was that I was defining my strengths through my own willingness to keep my personal gifts and strengths 'under wraps'. I came to a personal realization that unwrapping the gifts that I was tucking away was the beginning of an entirely new redefinition of who I was, and who I was going to be. So now it was decision time.

My first decision was to define those strengths inside myself, the ones I was protecting for so long. The first and most important gift was the ability to love myself, and to spread that love to other people. This one came directly from the promise I made to my mother. The next gift was brutal honesty. This is where I chose to go deep inside myself and find not only those things that needed to change, but the beauty I was hiding.

My last gift was my faith. Being that private person, I also kept my faith private. One's relationship with God, to some extent, is a private matter. On the other hand, defining my faith and then sharing it with others who are willing to listen was a huge step toward redefinition, and gave life to both my ability to love myself and others, and my willingness to share my gifts with them.

For many people, the defining measures of their lives are their birth, and their eventual death. But the real defining measure of a human being is to understand who we are, and why we are here. My mother's life, her passing, the promise I made to her and myself, and my willingness to follow through, set the stage for my ability to define who I am, and why I am here. I don't think there's anything that has been so poignant in my life.

> *The real defining measure of a human being is to understand who we are, and why we are here.*

Each day, I rise with a renewed commitment to continue to become the best version of myself that I can be, and to connect with other human beings who I am blessed to share this planet with. I understand that the reason I am here is to be in service of other people. No one becomes proficient at serving others until they understand who they are and their purpose in this world.

I have done many interviews since I began writing, and I am often asked this question: Who is Faust Ruggiero? Each time I answer that question, I reflect back to the choice I made to commit my life to become a loving person, and to extend my loving gifts outward to others who enter my world. When I answer that question, I talk about being a person in service to others, and the reciprocal growth that happens when we open ourselves up to the love that is inside us, and its potential to change the world we live in.

I am blessed each day to know that regardless of what happens in my world, it will be defined by my passion to express that love not only to myself, but to everyone I touch. Choices can be a wonderful thing. They are particularly fulfilling when they force us to challenge ourselves, accept the challenge, and grow into an entirely new human.

> *Choices can be a wonderful thing. They are particularly fulfilling when they force us to challenge ourselves, accept the challenge, and grow into an entirely new human.*

So, in this third chapter of my life, without reservation, I define my existence by my willingness to love, and the continuation of my life in service of other people. To love and to serve, as I understand it, is the pinnacle of human existence. It is higher order living at its best. Most important, it is a reciprocal gift. One never stops learning, giving, receiving, and in the end, the genuine purpose for why I am here is realized and lived every day of my life.

GRATEFUL FOR THE JOURNEY
~ FRANCES RAE KEY ~

WHAT A DELIGHT it is to share my story with those who are approaching or examining their 'third chapter' of life. The years we spend as elders can be such a wonderful, liberating, creative time if we open our hearts to it.

To lay the groundwork for understanding the course of my life: at the time of this writing, I'm seventy-one years of age. I was born in 1952 on the military base in Cuba to an Australian mother and an American father who met in Perth during WWII. I am the mother of four adult daughters, have seven grandchildren, and four great-grandchildren. I was married twice, and remarkably, I met both of my husbands at age fourteen. Even though we did not remain married, I was blessed to be asked to be by their sides when each of them passed away.

My profession in the past was that of a teacher. At various times in my life, I taught Language Arts to elementary and middle school children, as well as music and ESL (English as a Second Language) to refugees through Lutheran Social Services. I have always been involved in humanitarian kind of work and have a deep affinity for classical music and writing poetry, fiction, scripts, and more.

During my growing up years, my father was somewhat in the background of my life due to his depression, but I had an immutable bond with my mother, who was a dose of pure sunshine. She was a teacher, writer, and musician, and she opened a small private school when I was three years old so she could work and keep me at home with her. Until the day she died, I saw her or spoke to her almost every day of my life. I consider her to be my spiritual teacher and dearest friend.

My mother and I attended the Catholic church, which she had been raised in, but when I was about six years old, she left the church and began searching for other forms of inspiration. When I was around eight, I began to write poetry of a spiritual nature, and by the age of nine my mother and I were having in-depth discussions about various religions and ways of perceiving the Divine. My mother understood and guided me through the psychic experiences that were a natural, constant part of my life, and when I began to do a form of 'automatic writing', she was there to advise me. This exploration opened my mind greatly, but I have always maintained a deep love for and connection to Jesus. All of this certainly laid the groundwork for the rest of my life.

Around the age of fifty, I was heavily involved in writing music about peace and international goodwill for a chorus I had created called "The International Peace Performers." I came up with the idea for this group after working in a refugee camp for six weeks, a life-changing experience that healed me greatly of an earlier trauma I'd had in life, which had involved both physical and mental abuse. Interacting compassionately with people who had been through such extreme trauma put my experience in perspective and gave me an insight into the healing power of human kindness. While at the camp, I wrote a song for the youth to sing. It was, of all things, a song of gratitude for those who had helped them, and I saw firsthand the therapeutic value of music in healing trauma. This song, "The Children of Kosovo", opened the door to so much that was to follow in my life.

The International Peace Performers consisted of children in my hometown of Jacksonville, Florida who were refugees from many countries, along with American children. We had some fantastic voices in the group and were invited to sing at many events over the next six years. We worked with some professional arrangers who created gorgeous renditions of my songs, and I had the children record in excellent studios to produce some beautiful CDs.

In the year 2000, I pieced together these songs and created a musical out of them called *The Mountain of Peace*. The musical required over forty performers and told the story of six families from around the world who each lost a child to war and went on a journey to find the mythological Mountain of Peace. It was put on at several universities; other times, I produced the show myself. People were deeply moved each time we did it, and I felt my goal of inspiring people to think about solutions to war was achieved.

A number of choruses have performed my peace songs in schools and churches around the world, including the North Florida Democratic Inauguration Ball, the National Conference of the Department of Peace in Washington, DC, and the Jordanian Children's Chorus at the International UNICEF Conference. I was most honored when North America's Native American Elder Dave Courchene presented one of the songs on video at an Indigenous Round Table at the Capitol Building.

When I was fifty-six, I completed a musical called *Aussie Song*, which explored my mother's close bond with her father and a family deception that threatened to tear them apart, as well as her marriage to an American sailor in WWII and her immigration to the U.S. Shortly after I finished the musical, we learned Mother had lung cancer. When one of the local theaters who I'd given the script to contacted me about including it in their upcoming season, we were thrilled. My mother was able to see all ten shows at The Atlantic Beach Experimental Theatre before she passed away twenty months later.

On October 9, 2010, my mother's soul left her physical body. It was the greatest loss of my life. Because I'd often had dreams and spirit visitations from people who had died, I assumed that my mother would reach out to me from the Other Side – but I never imagined it would be in the manner in which it occurred. Nineteen days after her memorial, I was on an airplane to New York City to see my daughters, looking out over the heavenly clouds, and I posed a question to my mother in my mind, "Mother, is there any distance for you?" and I heard her answer me, both in my mind and audibly! Stunned, I began to write down the stream of information she gave me.

I thought this would be a one-time spiritual event in my life, but it continued for several years, resulting in four books. The first book was released three weeks after the communication had begun, another was released later that year, and the other two more gradually. I hand-wrote the books, feeling an energy flow as I wrote, and I soon realized that not only was my mother communicating with me, but an entire team of beings to whom she was connected. I named the books *The Team: A Mother's Wisdom from the Other Side* because her primary message was "You are not alone. You are not even functioning as one person. Nobody is, for you are a member of a team, a spiritual team as close to you as breathing."

In 2019, at the age of sixty-seven, I entered *Aussie Song* in a theater competition in NYC. To my great joy, we were nominated for Best Show and won Best Music. It was definitely one of the highlights of my life! I continue to promote the show in hopes that other theaters will pick it up and share it in a larger way. (Come on, Hugh Jackman!)

In 2022, I self-published a novel called *The Train to Hoffehausen* about the lives of two women from different generations who are actually reincarnations of one another, affecting each other's decisions. I held a book release event in NYC with some wonderful actors and singers who sang the theme song I wrote for the story. Since then, I have written a screenplay for a TV series based on this novel, which I continue to circulate through the film industry in hopes of seeing the story as a movie.

As you can see, the sixties for me were an incredibly busy time. At age sixty-two, I went to Australia by myself for a full month. I met relatives I'd never known and by train I traced my mother's travels as a child/teen, which took me all over the country. In a small town near Perth, I went up in a hot air balloon and released some of my mother's ashes. I tracked down several people who knew my mother as a child, and most amazingly, I located my grandfather's unmarked grave!

I lived in New York City in a studio apartment for three years so I could help with my grandchildren when their parents moved there, continuing to travel back and forth to Florida to my home to be with other family members. While there, I joined The New York Community Chorus, a truly wonderful experience. During my sixties, I was also blessed to be included in family trips to Spain, Italy, Portugal, Paris, Costa Rica, and Vieques in Puerto Rico, to name a few.

In my late sixties, I had two close brushes with death/disability and came through both unscathed. At age sixty-seven, doctors found a brain aneurysm, and I had immediate surgery. However, when they went into the place where *three* specialists had seen the aneurysm on the scan, it was gone. I wasn't surprised – while under anesthesia, I saw a group of angels who told me that I would be fine, and indeed I was. The doctors were shocked, unable to give an explanation.

The next year, I had three profound, detailed dreams where I was shown that I would soon die in a car accident. The dream involved these elements: my sister saying to me, *"You paused, and it changed your destiny,"* my deceased husband greeting me and saying I had died and he was going to escort me to the Other Side, and me arguing my case to stay, even making a written list of things I needed to complete on earth (I remember only three things on the list). Because of the many other dreams and visions I'd had in life, I knew this dream was a true prediction.

A week later, I was driving past a building at 11:00 p.m. that had once been a metaphysical church my mother and I had attended many years before. This church had been very important in both our lives. Despite the late hour, the large veranda was all lit up with brilliant lamps. A group of about fifteen people with white, glowing hair, presumably all elderly, were sitting and standing on the veranda. The sight was so strange and out-of-place that I slowed down to observe it for a few seconds. As I continued down the road, a car barreled through the stoplight and missed me by a millimeter. I had truly *"paused and changed my destiny."*

Not long after, my friend, Kathy, insisted that what I'd seen on that veranda were angels sent to protect me and suggested we go to the building and investigate what I saw that night. We went and talked to the owner of the house – and the neighbor as well – and learned that there were no people on the veranda that night or any other night. The house belonged to an elderly couple and theirs was a quiet residential area. This vision was just that – a vision of glowing-haired beings designed to cause me to pause and miss the traffic accident.

The neighbor who was part of the discussion with the owner was a physician at the Mayo Clinic. When I decided to write about this experience in my book *In the Company of Souls*, he gave me permission to use his name as verification that what I'd seen had not been of the physical world. Whether my own soul created this vision or whether my Spiritual Team made an appearance on that veranda, I don't know, but their mission to help me remain in the physical world was accomplished.

My seventieth birthday party in October, 2022 was magnificent, a lovefest of friends and family. I truly felt I was floating in another dimension that night. One of my daughters had everyone paint something on a large canvas as a memento. This was an amazing surprise since three months prior, a medium had told me she saw my Team reaching out to give me a 'boost' in the form of a painting made by many hands. She said it was 'from Spirit' but involved human hands, too. What a beautiful confirmation of the love of those on the Other Side. Shortly after my birthday, I released another book, *In the Company of Souls*, a compilation of psychic, intuitive, and spiritual experiences that I and other close friends and family members have had throughout our lives.

What is ahead for me as I go through my seventies? I have no doubt my life will contain many more ups and downs, for this is the natural pace of life. My truth has become very simple as I age: to greet each situation that presents itself to me as the one I am meant to have, and to make it a little better than how I find it... to send out pre-forgiveness into each day ahead of myself so I do not fall into judgment... to be an example to the children in my life of what I hope they will model... to examine my heart and mind carefully to see where I contribute to negative conditions in the world so I can correct myself... and to stay in a mindset of *gratitude*. I ask, each day, to be a good steward of the material that was entrusted to me by my spiritual Team and to use the gift of the extra time that's been granted to me very wisely. Sometimes, I manage to do these things – other times, I don't.

> *My truth has become very simple as I age: to greet each situation that presents itself to me as the one I am meant to have, and to make it a little better than how I find it...*

These are, in summary, the outward and inward events of my life. By far, the most important gain I have made is an inner awareness of the Divine, which is present in everything. Any outer achievements I've made have only been a means to this end. The Team Books teach that when we pass away, the various roles we played in life fade away like a dream. All we keep is the love we've given and allowed others to give us. This Third Chapter has allowed me more time to learn and to teach these life principles; I'm so thankful for the privilege of living it.

LIVING MY BEST LIFE
~ ROZ WEINBERGER ~

AS I LOOK at my life and history now from the perspective of being in my third chapter, I realize I need to wake up each morning with a smile. It can be difficult but I need to try – it gives me a focus.

My parents left Hungary and survived the Holocaust. My grandparents did not, they were murdered in Auschwitz. My parents met and were then married in 1942 in Belgium and went directly into hiding. They never saw their parents and some siblings again. I relate this story so you can understand where I came from and how my brother and I grew up with parents who suffered from survivors' guilt and ghosts.

In 1950, my parents and brother left Europe for Canada, where I was born in Montreal, Quebec, Canada. I was barely a toddler when our family moved to the United States, where I grew up and became integrated into a culture that my family found both foreign and ultimately familiar. But my parents were determined to 'fit in' and our family assimilated and ultimately thrived in our adopted homeland.

Fast forward a few years and I was, to say the least, 'adventuresome'. In addition, I was an American kid living in an Eastern European family, which had its challenges. I'm not sure if it was my innate need to find adventure, or my need for freedom. All I know is that I had a clear need and it took me in many directions over the years. I went to college and received a BA in Political Science, which didn't count for much of anything at the time unless law school was a goal. I left for Israel two weeks after graduation. I was brought up to be a Zionist, which I still am today. As a Zionist, it made sense to go to Israel.

I worked as an Immigration Specialist for the Israeli government for a year, got married to a college friend and we lived on kibbutz (agricultural commune) for a year. We returned to the U.S. after that; it was the time to be near family. We were married for eighteen years and had two children before it became clear that we needed to go back to being just friends. My ex-husband has always been a 'mensch', we had an amicable divorce and remain friends. He has always done the right thing for his family; I even like his present wife.

I went back to work and had many 'mini' careers. I worked at a state agency, went to NYU for Social Work, but the statistic course scared me into leaving. In those days, it wouldn't have paid the loans back. Social workers just weren't valued, despite their core values of supporting the dignity of individuals and recognizing their values and the importance of human relationships.

I then ran the business end of a Martial Arts studio, sold junk bonds, opened a Jewish education poster company, and worked in corporate for a furniture chain. Apparently, my passion for immigration was under the skin because I obtained a position in a tech company in their immigration department. I worked on out-bound visas and had the opportunity to lecture to our associates on immigration all over North and South America. I retired from corporate in 2016 thinking I had had enough of working and I needed some down time.

At that point, I just couldn't see myself reinventing my life, so I turned to my long-time passion and hobby: pottery making. I launched a pottery business Roz Potz from my home. While my ceramic pottery creations were beautiful and popular and attracted positive reviews, it quickly became clear that the business couldn't pay all the bills. Necessity being the mother of invention, I realized my pottery-making passion was not going to support my family. Time to find a Plan B.

Over the years, I had gained a fair bit of weight. About the time Covid 19 hit, I realized I needed to lose some serious weight, which I did by working out six days a week and pushing my aging body to achieve a level of fitness that surprised even me. Friends and acquaintances noticed too, and I began helping others find their path to fitness and wellness and obtained my Personal Training license.

I also took on a job as the Assistant Property Manager of my condo complex during Covid while my personal training client list grew.

As a property manager, I'm a very customer-oriented person and this work suits me perfectly. I work about twenty hours a week and also offer personal training to a number of people, including my dear friend Irene Weinberg. I'm one of those people who have lots of energy and can juggle a number of tasks pretty much simultaneously. It's a great strength to have in my property management work. And it's especially helpful as I now live in a three-generation household with two very energetic teenage grandsons.

I started living in a mother-daughter home with my daughter, who is an educator, and her children about seven years ago. My daughter divorced several years ago due to a nearly tragic domestic incident. She and her twin children aged twelve were involved in a domestic violence incident. A divorce followed. Our family is still healing from that experience.

> *"The future belongs to those who believe in the beauty of their dreams."*
> —Eleanor Roosevelt

As I look at my life at this stage, I see that my ancestors, myself, and my family have managed not only to survive but to thrive. It hasn't been easy by any means. Our collective family experiences have not always been positive. We've come to realize that life just doesn't work that way. But, as a woman, a mother, a grandmother, artist, community activist, and just plain hard-working person with the usual pile of bills, I have persevered.

One of the many mantras that has helped me over the years came from the iconic Eleanor Roosevelt: "The future belongs to those who believe in the beauty of their dreams."

That is me, I like to encourage people and take a positive approach that helps people move forward and build on their strengths. It's like so many aspects of life and living: approaching life with a certain amount of optimism and hope will achieve so much more than poking and prodding people who may be reticent about trusting their abilities.

I must admit though that I hoped and believed life would be slower and with less drama as I got older. Hasn't happened. Of course, it was unlikely to be, with teenagers in my daily life. But seriously, I've found that those who expect life to slow down and hold less drama can grow old quickly.

Those who stop learning start to rot.

I believe it's all about attitude. Some days are easier than others. And yes, some days are downright tough to get through. I believe when the going gets tough, the tough get going. When you have that kind of attitude, it's hard to beat. I also found that a smile and laughter go a long way for the giver and the receiver.

Add to that a network of supportive family and friends; a mind open to new learning and experiences; and a belief that we can each make a difference; and you have a recipe for a happier life – at any age.

A WORK IN PROGRESS
~ MARY METCALFE ~

LIKE MANY OF the Baby Boom generation, I was raised in part by a World War II veteran and by my paternal grandparents. My father returned from the war with PTSD, a Traumatic Brain Injury (TBI), and chronic spinal injuries thanks to a grenade that left him with shrapnel in his head and spine for the rest of his short life. In those days, there was no diagnosis or treatment or even a name for Post-Traumatic Stress Disorder. For the TBI, there were only addictive narcotic pain killers added to buckets of alcohol at the local Legion.

My father was in no shape to be one. His gentle high school sweetheart wife divorced him. His second wife, my mother, left him before I was three after relentless physical and emotional abuse and the stillborn death of my baby brother.

> "Until you make the unconscious conscious, it will direct your life and you will call it fate."
> —Carl Jung

At three, I started living with my grandparents and spending holidays with my father and his common-law partner, who wasn't interested in raising "someone else's brat". At five, I was hit by a car and spent over a month in hospital with a double compound skull fracture and more months in a hospital bed in the livingroom.

At seven, my grandparents sold their beautiful three-bedroom home and moved to a one-bedroom apartment. I spent Christmas 1961 with neighbors. My father refused to take me and my grandparents were hoping not to.

From that point forward, I never had a bedroom or bed of my own. For years, I slept in a sleeping bag on a folding lounge chair in my grandparents' dining room or on a couch or a camp cot depending on where my father was living. For several months in 1965 at the age of eleven, I slept in the same bed as my father. That didn't end well. I turned up at my grandparents' apartment in the middle of the night. That was followed by a trip to a 'gynecologist' to prove I wasn't, as my father claimed, 'promiscuous.' I clearly remember the doctor's words: "The hymen is intact." I was never allowed to live alone with him again.

My seriously depressed diabetic grandmother died of a stroke in August 1970, just seven weeks before my father in early October. He was just forty-nine. Both of them had a very authoritarian view of parenting. There was little praise and lots of punishment, including punching, slapping, spanking, and withholding food. There were days I couldn't go to school because of visible injuries.

I learned that the only way to get any recognition was to become a super-achiever. It worked until my grades fell below the honors level because of our troubles at home, which sometimes included the police late at night. Those last two years were hell on very little sleep.

Fast forward and I continued to try to be everything and do everything: full-time high school, part-time job, vice-president and then president of the high school student council, president of our youth church group. By 1972, I was in university and still trying to do it all.

In 1974, I transferred universities and moved away from my grandfather. I chafed at his restrictions. He was never abusive in any way, but I was young, angry, and emotionally damaged.

My grandfather and I eventually became loving family after I moved out. But not before family and family friends called me selfish and ungrateful. However, I was determined to make my own way in the world so off I went. My "Bompa" cheered me on my way and helped pay my tuition for the next two years.

After graduating a four-year Journalism program with honors, I put on a convincing act. My career took off in leaps and bounds. But, so did my anxiety. I had panic attacks at work and being in line at the bank. I developed what I now recognize as "Imposter Syndrome". I was convinced that people would eventually realize I was faking my skills and abilities. So, I worked even harder and took on 'special projects' that involved long hours.

In spring 1981, I finally quit a public relations job that had me travelling away from home almost every weekend over the competitive ski season. I was burned out, depressed, and concerned for my marriage. Something had to give.

In the fall of 1981, my beloved 90-year-old grandfather passed on within a week of me learning I was pregnant. He had been a loving constant in my life and had always done his best to assure me that I was a good person and worthy of love. His words made me feel better but the negative childhood scripts constantly running in the background wouldn't go away. That would take another forty years.

In May 1982, our beautiful daughter was born. My husband Jacques and I were thrilled and whisked her away to our lovely country home where I had decorated her bedroom next to ours. I worried I wouldn't be able to handle a baby but she taught me each day and many nights. Somehow, we both survived with lots of cuddles and times of confused clinging to each other.

Unfortunately, I went back to my government contract work after four months and went right back into super-achiever mode. I worked through a bout of pneumonia. Later, I was hospitalized for a week and unable to work for a month following a serious staph infection.

By this time, I was a senior partner in a small but growing management consulting firm. The founding partner was not especially supportive of women in the workforce, so I just worked harder to make less money than him and the two other male partners. I was actually told that since my husband worked and their wives didn't, I didn't need a raise, let alone pay equity.

After carrying the company payroll for two months when accounts receivable went behind, I quit and started my own company.

When my former partner called me and falsely accused me of bad-mouthing the company, I challenged him: "Tell me who said what and I can respond. Otherwise, this is just innuendo." That was the last I heard from him.

Throughout these months and years, it became increasingly clear to me that I needed serious counselling. I'd learned that many of my problems with self-esteem, periodic depression, periodic insomnia, and anxiety could be attributed to being an Adult Child of An Alcoholic (ACOA), aka my father.

Then there was *my* PTSD. First officially recognized in 1980, PTSD was still not well recognized in the affected individuals, let alone its impacts on entire families. That was still years away, as was effective counselling and treatment. Even less known was C-PTSD or Complex PTSD. It was first coined in 1992 and is still to this day only gradually making its way into mainstream consciousness.

> Over the years, not one even mentioned PTSD let alone C-PTSD. I honestly believe some of them thought I was just some over-achieving middle class woman who liked the thought of being 'in therapy'.

In my case, a succession of counsellors told me I was coping well. Over the years, not one even mentioned PTSD let alone C-PTSD. I honestly believe some of them thought I was just some over-achieving middle class woman who liked the thought of being 'in therapy'. I had sat in hotel ballrooms all day learning about 'self-esteem'. I had collections of tapes on affirmations, and meditations that were all the rage. I even had subliminal tapes. I didn't know what they were telling my sub-conscious; I only knew I was still depressed and anxious and periodically self-medicating with way too much wine.

Over those years, I tried to be the parent to our daughter that I never had. Our daughter went to private Montessori school up to middle school. We bought a beautiful house with an in-ground swimming pool. We had mother-daughter trips to Mexico, Jamaica, Vermont, and New York. I coached her bowling team. My husband and I sponsored and coached her high school softball team. We never felt we were helicopter parents. We just wanted our daughter to feel we were there for her.

Only many years later did we learn that she didn't feel I was "emotionally available". At the time, I didn't know what she meant by that because she wouldn't discuss it. We went to a therapist of her choice in 2016 and listened for an hour. Even after further remote sessions, we couldn't find any path forward. It's only now that I realize I couldn't be adequately emotionally available for her because I wasn't available for myself. I subsequently worked with an energy healer and counsellor for the better part of a year and felt I was making real progress.

But by May 2018, when our grandson was six years old, I was diagnosed with congestive heart failure, brought on by chemotherapy years earlier for breast cancer. I had been born with a mild congenital defect in my heart, which eighteen months of chemo brought to the fore. After a week in hospital, I was sent home with a pile of prescriptions to take for the rest of my life and exercise-induced chronic fatigue. Our daughter came up from Houston for a family get-together that July. She said it was a "deposit in the relationship bank". So far, so good. She offered to call more regularly and send samples of our grandson's artwork. Great!

Except nothing happened.

In early October 2018, I had an angiogram that showed my heart wasn't yet "bad enough" for corrective surgery. At this point, I had severe vertigo. I was having panic attacks. I quickly became even more deeply depressed. I was pre-diabetic. We hadn't heard anything from our daughter for weeks. I careened down the rabbit hole.

I woke up in the hospital. I had overdosed on Ativan, which I learned was not at a dosage high enough to kill me. It was, however, enough to finally get me the help I needed. The psychiatrist prescribed a low-dose antidepressant. Within weeks, I was a new person: vertigo gone, anxiety gone, depression fading, and feelings of being overwhelmed subsided.

I decided to give myself and my life another chance, with or without our daughter in it. I knew I had a long road ahead but for the first time in decades I felt up to the task. I was sixty-four.

In the past five years, I have gradually come to terms with my past, my present, and I hope, my future. In the process, I've come to like myself, flaws and all. Our daughter spent several months in 2019 and 2020 lobbing email diagnoses at me: Narcissist, Borderline Personality Disorder, Bipolar Disorder, explosive temper (?), not emotionally available, can't keep friends (several for over 45 years?) and on and on. I finally realized she was gaslighting me; trying to make me question my sanity. When I reached out for support to my older and younger half-sisters and a dear cousin, she said it was "inappropriate" and "trying to justify" my (PTSD-triggered) behavior (anxiety and depression). When I responded that neither my family doctor nor psychiatrist agreed to even assess for any of her labels, she went "no contact".

> In the past five years, I have gradually come to terms with my past, my present, and I hope, my future. In the process, I've come to like myself, flaws and all.

She laid out terms, some of which made no sense to any of the professionals I've been working with. For example, she wanted her father and I to do months of intensive "family systems therapy" but wouldn't participate herself, despite the clear family triangle with her being an only child. Her conditions went on and on. None of them included her participation. We realized she was dealing with her own mental health issues and wasn't ready. She blocked us on all social media. She refused to let us visit with our grandson or his baby sister. No contact. Period.

At first, I was optimistic we could find a way forward and, through our son-in-law, offered approaches I'd researched through peer-reviewed literature. Didn't work.

I have now come to accept that I will always love our daughter but we will likely never be friends. Our grandchildren don't know us, which is very sad. But, I am building some family history for them for when they are old enough to make their own judgments.

We went through a long three years of grieving, even as I worked on my issues and came to terms with my 'triggers' around abandonment and learning to love myself. I joined a group of over 3,000 estranged mothers. They have helped me realize I am not alone in thinking I did the best I could with what I knew at the time.

Now, I wake up each day with gratitude, hope for myself, and for our world. I actively try to do some good each and every day. I remain engaged in what is going on in the world around me. I have to put all the negatives into perspective but I try to "think global and act local".

In January 2023, I decided to fold up my editing/publishing company, intending to retire. However, the universe clearly has other ideas. Hence, this book and this project and a few others that are developing.

I have come to realize that *mistakes are learning opportunities*; my so-called 'failures' have always taught me new approaches. Throughout my life, I have always tried to respect and have compassion for all those I've come in contact with, including those with mental health issues.

A few months ago, I wrote my son-in-law to keep the door open with our daughter with one caveat: we deserve to be treated with respect.

And my father? For decades after he died in 1970, I tried to hate him and what he'd done to me. A small voice reminded me that there were many times when he was a good father. Once I understood PTSD and TBI, I realized he couldn't control his outbursts and hallucinations.

I have since come to terms with his legacy. When we meet in heaven, it will be with warm love, compassion, and understanding. I now understand how PTSD and TBI changed his world and reality and mine as well. There was no malice. And somewhere, there was love.

I remain optimistic that I am here to fulfill a purpose larger than me or my life. I have faith that the universe isn't finished with me yet.

I am a work in progress – building my strength and resiliency each day to be able to help myself, humanity, and the natural world around us.

WE'RE NEVER TOO OLD TO BE PART OF THE SOLUTION
ROBERT (BOB) WELLS

I ENTERED THE THIRD chapter of my life almost completely unprepared for the loss of stamina, strength, balance, walking, and ability to do everyday things that needed doing. I always thought it would take longer to grow old.

Now, at eighty-seven years of age, I know first-hand that growing older can be a devastating experience. In 2017, when we sold our home and car and I got rid of my boat, all my fishing and hunting equipment and moved into a retirement residence it was clearly life-altering. At the time, Inge, my wife of sixty years had lost most of her eyesight, was almost completely deaf, and had rapidly progressing dementia. I had a heart attack in 2021 and spent seven months in hospital as she continued to decline. We were never to live together again. In 2022, she passed on in her ninetieth year, ending our sixty-two-year loving marriage.

I have now been living in long-term care for the past two years. I use a wheelchair to get around and cannot get in or out of bed without help. But, I keep busy and positive with the help of staff, family, and many friends. Recently, I have become very interested in learning more about Climate Change, sharing that knowledge and encouraging other seniors to engage in research, discussion, and sharing their views and ideas. Through it all, I remain convinced that many older people can provide a wealth of wisdom for young people, their organizations, and society.

A little history will help you understand my lifelong and continuing passionate involvement in nature and our environment. In 1938, my parents purchased property on Windigoostigwan Lake in Northwestern Ontario from Professor Frank Buck, an uncle of renowned author Pearl S. Buck. They built Wells' Fishing and Hunting Lodge at Mile Post 104 – denoting the number of miles along the Canadian National Railroad (CNR) track between Port Arthur and Fort William (now known as the amalgamated city of Thunder Bay).

Our family consisted of my mom and dad, three younger brothers, and myself. During the winter we lived in relative solitude close to nature. There were no roads or automobiles. I never met children who lived more than twenty miles away.

My parents permitted me the independence to wander, free from fear and the prevalent racial, religious, and ethnic prejudices. Becoming everyone's regular drop-in visitor, my dog Bernie at my side and .22-calibre rifle in hand, I roamed wherever my legs would take me.

In time, American doctors, automotive executives, and businessmen were arriving and leaving weekly by train. Exceptionally good fishing, home-cooked meals, kerosene lamps, and good service brought "tourists" back year after year to fish and or hunt.

At age nine, I made a 'sacred promise' to my Indigenous friend *Moochum* (Grandfather) Joe that I would live my life and then "draw words on paper" to tell

> We humans are neither more nor less than one part of a vast and critically interconnected natural world.

my kind how badly Indigenous people are/were treated and that all peoples must stop abusing Mother Nature – "We are one."

Moochum Joe was an Anishinabek Elder, who, along with my Anglo-Christian parents, was one of my important teachers about life and living. In those days, many white people thought Moochum Joe to be an "illiterate and lazy old Indian" – he was anything but! He was my dear friend and an unforgettable teacher. He taught me to observe and learn from all my senses. He helped me know that I was loved. And, he taught me to know and respect Mother Nature.

Through him and others, I grew to understand that we humans are neither more nor less than one part of a vast and critically interconnected natural world. In contrast, most white people in my youth believed that Canada was a challenging wilderness to triumph over and that pushing aside the Indigenous residents was their imperialist and divine right.

I grew up in the 1930s, 40s and 50s along the southern end of Canada's boreal forest. After completing high school, I chose to remain close to nature and became a fishing/hunting guide, forest fire fighter, fur trapper, and had a 30-year career as a Forest Technician/Conservation Officer with the Ontario Ministry of Natural Resources.

Forests play an important role in mitigating the climate crisis. The boreal forest is a green swath that sweeps around the Northern Hemisphere from Canada across to Scandinavia via Russia, to the northern tip of Japan, back to Alaska and Canada. The boreal forest is the largest terrestrial biome on the planet. There is more carbon stored in and under the lakes, in the forests, and the bogs of the boreal forest than is in the atmosphere itself. The increasingly intense storm systems, devastating droughts, torrential rains, wildfires, melting glaciers, rising sea levels, and dangerously high temperatures are endangering life in every corner of the planet – on the land, in the water, and in the atmosphere. The boreal forests, like all forest trees, are a critical factor in mitigating climate changes.

Canada is home to 630 Indigenous communities who have lived on and deeply understand the land, forests, and lakes over thousands of years and long before the arrival of white settlers. Indigenous peoples today are on the frontlines of the climate crisis. Indigenous voices have not only sounded the alarm about the dramatic changes they're witnessing, but they are also stepping forward to share their knowledge and experience.

I believe we have become very disconnected from the natural world and many of us have an egocentric world view: the belief that we are the center of the universe. I think we fear the idea of personal change because we might have to give up something. However, human beings at their best, are creative and inventive. I believe that when we have compassion and humility as our guiding principles, we can create, develop, and implement systems of change that are beneficial to all sentient beings, nature, and the environment.

> *I believe we have become very disconnected from the natural world and many of us have an egocentric world view: the belief that we are the center of the universe.*

I now live in a nursing home in Ottawa, the capital of Canada. Here, I have started a "Talking Circle" of seniors that meet monthly. Talking circles have been used for generations by Indigenous peoples to come together with mutual respect and civility to discuss issues that affect the entire community, including nature. One recurring theme now continues to be Climate Change.

We are never too old to become involved. We all have a shared interest. Save Mother Earth by using your voice! Addressing climate change requires weaving science, climate, biodiversity, equity, and human dignity into a seamless tapestry of action, policy, and transformation. We must do all we can to address this climate crisis. We need to set aside ego, pride, and greed. We owe it to ourselves, our grandchildren, and the generations to come.

If you've read this far, it's because you care about what happens to our planet and hopefully you want to be part of the solution.

Finding those solutions means working together and breaking down systemic barriers. Indigenous Peoples have made and will continue to make a remarkable comeback. Non-Indigenous Americans and Canadians have a choice to make: stand in the way or be part of a new narrative. All of us can and need to create a world different from the past. To succeed, we must consider Mother Nature in all that we do. We must change the conversation – shift the focus from doom and gloom to opportunity and possibility. Every person needs to understand and embrace their personal and unique role in the change.

Those of us in the third chapters of our lives need to help change the conversation about climate change. We must stay engaged to the best of our abilities.

The future, if we have one, will judge us on the history we create today – no matter our age.

BECOMING A WISE ONE
EMBRACING AND CELEBRATING LATER STAGES OF YOUR EARTHLY EXPERIENCE

~ **MARK PITSTICK** ~

A DMITTEDLY, THERE ARE some downsides at age seventy: baldness, hearing aids, dental crowns, and more. However, I've learned to focus on the positive; to *always reach for the highest feeling thought*. In that spirit, I'll share eight of the blessings I am experiencing in the final third of my awesome visit to this planet. I hope that reading about mine will help you consider yours, focus on your strengths, awaken from spiritual amnesia, and share your greatest gifts. You never know – you might be 'the 100th monkey' who helps many people and our planet reach a breakthrough.[3]

---

[3] Note: free articles at SoulProof.com website providing additional information are noted by #__

1. Learning the Rules of Life's Game

I enjoy playing *Monopoly* and *Sorry* and other games with my grandchildren. Invariably, we have to look at the rulebook since, after all, how can you play a game without knowing the rules? Your time of visiting earth is the same way.

In my youth, I purposely tried to understand how most humans think and how I could optimally function among them. I felt like a stranger in a strange land – a phrase I later learned when reading Robert Heinlein's classic book. Some of my conclusions about the rules of living on earth . . .

a. *People are doing the best they can,* given their degree of consciousness, beliefs, background, and resources.

b. Everyone is different and should get credit for just showing up on earth, let alone staying here. If you ask and listen, you'll learn that everyone has amazing stories to tell. As such, *I try to not judge anyone or assume I know how it is for them.*

c. No matter what I say and do, I won't please everyone so I should speak my highest truths and follow my inner dictates.

d. We flourish when we pursue what interests us AND serves others.

e. I only have one body/brain so it's wise to care for the temple of my soul.

f. We each have higher-energy assistants/assistance that guide and support us, especially when we ask for it and follow that 'small still voice' within.

Learning these and other 'rules' about how to play the game of life while on earth have benefited me greatly and saved me much time, energy, and stress. (#19 and 58)

2. Realizing the Big Picture of Life

Early on, I realized that beliefs of people and organizations differed widely. Those differences involved religious beliefs, political affiliations, life philosophies, and other key areas. I saw that some people blindly and/or automatically adopted views of their family, community, and church. They weren't open-minded about others outside their 'tribe'.

For example, I attended a fundamentalist church at age eighteen for the most important reason of all: my girlfriend went there. This exposed me to extreme examples of beliefs and doctrines that, somehow, people swallowed. They had no problem accepting that God, whose love was much greater than that of any earthly parent, would delegate the majority of His children to a fiery place of torment forever. Fortunately, my time at that church and its cultish close-minded believers was limited.

One blessing of that experience was it motivated me to deeply consider what I thought were *key teachings of Jesus and other great spiritual teachers*. Those include love your neighbor AND yourself, know that God loves and assists you, and fulfill your highest purposes. Other key takeaways included: this earthly experience is like a race so do your best, know that life continues after your body dies, and spend some time each day in prayer and contemplation.

I now experience high levels of peace, joy, love, gratitude, enthusiasm, and other higher energies/emotions/ways of being. That, in part, is because I've been able to distill human understandings and focus on what I consider to be the big picture of life. (#68 and 72)

3. Benefiting from Cumulative Self-Care and Awareness Practices

For the most part, I quickly gravitated to exemplary habits during my younger years. After reading for hours, I noticed how good it felt to stretch in different ways. Later, I discovered the science of yoga and have practiced that discipline for fifty years. At age nineteen, while looking at a poster advertising meditation classes, *my intuition said*: 'You should go to that.' I've enjoyed the practice and advantages of yoga ever since. At age twenty-one, a law passed that required food manufacturers to list ingredients in processed foods. As I read the description of what was in baloney – which had been a common part of my diet – I knew it was time to take that off my grocery list. (It's not a good sign when pig's ears and sheep's lips are the first two items.)

Over time, I fine-tuned my exercise program, rest, inner cleansing, and other key factors for optimal wellness. All this has allowed me to optimize my body, brain, and consciousness. This allows me to enjoy – nearly all the time – a heavenly life NOW no matter what is happening to me or around me. Further, I know that *the quality of my afterlife experience will be a reflection of my consciousness when I change worlds.* Finally, my way of being directly assists others. In the last decade especially, a number of people have said: "Your printed and spoken words are wonderful, but your personal energy helps me the most." (#12, 77, and 87)

4. Honoring and Learning from The Past

In my youth, I often chastised myself about how I could have done better. (That was a lower-energy habit that I picked up from family and friends.) That habit, needless to say, serves no one and wastes precious time and energy. From my current elder perspective, I strive to catch those self-sapping and zapping thoughts. Then I quickly replace them with higher-energy ones that involve the following keys: (#41, 79, and 108)

a. Realize that berating myself isn't fair since hindsight is 20/20. I did my best considering what I knew and how I was at the time.

b. Acknowledge that a brief review of when 'I missed the mark' – the original Aramaic meaning of the word 'sin' – helps me learn and improve.

c. Highlight all the good and great things I've done instead of excessively revisiting the relatively few areas where I didn't.

d. Know that I learned a lot from my 'mistakes' and remember that, with the right perspective, those can help me and others.

e. Bless earlier aspects of myself, praise my efforts, and set the intention that I will do better in the future.

5. Hearing and Following My Inner Knowing

This is one of the coolest parts of being older, at least in this time-space slice of life. Learning how to discern the wisdom of my higher self didn't come easily for me. (That may be because I have such an active mental sphere, am super busy, and am quite bull-

> *After many instances of being hit in the head by a cosmic two-by-four, I became more motivated to sense that inner guidance and follow its wise advice.*

headed.) To my credit, that still small voice can be difficult to notice. For me, it's subtle and fleeting so it was difficult to catch and trust.

However, after many instances of being hit in the head by a cosmic two-by-four, I became more motivated to sense that inner guidance and follow its wise advice. My fiancée Andy Lee – one of the most evolved persons I've met and an exemplary service provider as an RN, evidential medium, acupuncturist, and more – and I have discussed this topic many times. We agree that all the challenges of this earthly experience are easily worth the price of developing more rapid detection and following our inner knowing. That is an eternal benefit that becomes part of who we are and how we operate. (#51, 71, and 117)

6. Walking Daily with Creator

In my earlier days, I viewed Source as being separate from me. Before that, I had quickly discarded images from the Dark Ages that depicted God as a big judgmental and angry guy in the sky. Even so, it took many years to 'grok' that I really am an integral, infinite (ever-expanding), and beloved part of All That Is. That's a huge step from my earlier fundamentalist teachings that humans are ignorant and worthless sinners who need an intermediary to be saved.

The peace and joy that accompanies this realization is indescribable, especially as it becomes more internalized and obvious every year. I hope you increasingly feel what our Lutheran minister described in his *Benediction*: *May your heart and mind know the peace that passes all understanding.* (#13 and 73)

7. Making My Life a Work of Art

Another incredible part of this stage of life is realizing that I really can enjoy the greatest life that I have envisioned. (In this case, 'I' refers to the totality of my being – all the energy, awareness, information, and consciousness that I AM.) For most people, this includes mastering your personal life and shining brightly – as the old church hymn encouraged –to brighten the corner where you are. (#14 and 21)

8. Knowing That Life Doesn't End When This Earth-Suit Dies and Living Accordingly

Fully embracing and benefiting from one's later years on earth is much easier when you know that your real self is much more than this mortal earthly body. Much scientific, clinical, and experiential evidence now clearly shows that bodily death is NOT the end of life. That's the great news that sets us free and allows us to enjoy every stage of life. With this resolute knowledge, you can fully celebrate your youth, middle age, and advanced years fully. (#1, 60, 113, and 115)

> Much scientific, clinical, and experiential evidence now clearly shows that bodily death is NOT the end of life. That's the great news that sets us free and allows us to enjoy every stage of life.

I hope this article helps you cherish your current stage of life and create the most wonderful life of your dreams, not despite but because of your age. Please note that the eight verbs used – **learning, realizing, benefiting, honoring, hearing, walking, making, and knowing** – are in present participle form. (For those who took English several centuries ago like I did, verbs ending in 'ing' denote ongoing action.) This verb usage reminds us that *becoming a wise one is a journey, a process that doesn't end until we fully know and show our true natures in every moment.* That's when we realize there never really was anything we had to do since we were part of G.O.D. all the time.

MY PATH TO JOY

～ ANITA ALBRIGHT ～

HAVE YOU EVER given a gift? How did you feel when the person was not happy to receive it? Feel that. I now hold this vision: Everything that comes may not appear as a gift, but I accept and welcome it. When I remove the ugly wrapping paper and open it, I find the beautiful gifts my heart has longed for. I see everything as a gift, even the death or disease of a loved one. The moment it comes, I welcome it. It took some time to get this. It works! Once I got it, it was a relearning process; eventually, nothing moved me off my center. I bend like a tree when the wind blows. I feel it. I get the message from the feeling. It takes practice. It makes all the difference in how things unfold. You are about to read the story of my life's most potent transformative blessing: my journey to joy!

To write about the third chapter of my Life, I must briefly include the themes of my first two chapters. The first chapter of my life was with my family of origin, where I learned God was love and that I liked peace. In chapter two, I awakened to the spirit: taking responsibility, doing the right thing, and living from my highest vision became my way of life. I incorporated love and light into everything I met, including my home and work life. I could face all my challenges in that light. I loved my life!

That brings me to the third chapter of my Life. The third chapter happened when I was sixty-six, and it threw me for a loop because nothing I knew from the first two chapters could get me out of the *Big Grief*. In my story, you will learn how I am maneuvering through the third chapter of my Life: how I became friends with Grief, what I learned, and how I managed it. It is my path to joy.

The biggest realization I received at the onset of my path to joy was this: everyone is on their own journey, even our children. What I tell you here is what I did. It doesn't necessarily mean it works for you. It is my journey. It was designed especially for me. You will have your journey.

When a loved one 'dies' and this person has been a daily part of your Life, Grief shows up, ferociously leveling you. This person came through your birth canal. You nursed this person as a baby. You fed, bathed, taught, laughed, and cried with this person. You watched this person grow and develop into a positive, loving being. This person was a bright light in your life. You watched this person face and handle with integrity as best as possible all the earthly struggles: accidents, divorce, men, single parenting two sons and struggles with finances. You saw this person have one victory after another, facing these struggles and being a light in her world with almost everyone she met. You get a clue that your cord of connection is beyond just an earthly one.

In the last year of this person's life, this person graduated from college with honors. This person taught 6th grade Science, Math, and Mindfulness. This person loved nature and the outdoors. In two separate incidents, I saw her rescue an injured hawk and an uncrewed motorboat on the lake. She liked fermenting foods, eating salads, and raw garlic too. She camped, hiked, backpacked, paddle boarded, kayaked, played basketball, and made jewelry and salves. She loved her sons more than anything else in the world. She loved children, and children loved her. She had this unique way about her; whatever she got became beautiful, unique, and valuable. She was beautiful and radiant. She had perfect posture. She never met a stranger. She was independent. I could go on and on.

I love this person so much! This person is my daughter, Bonnie Jeanne Albright. I felt this deep, dark, empty place within myself. I felt like I could not go on without her. I was living without her Bonnie form on earth. For a time, I could do very little.

Don't feel sorry for me. It is what it is. The thought of Bonnie being gone left me lifeless. My body froze. My body was a walking gravestone. I had many things to deal with and needed support. Included in this list were Bonnie's two sons, my physical health, my disabled daughter, and coping with daily life under the strain of Grief. I had to heal myself. I had other children and my grandchildren. I had to get back into life. I am not a victim, so I embrace what is. I came to know that love never dies. Love is eternal. Bonnie was ever present with me. Changing my thinking, I began to heal.

> I came to know that love never dies. Love is eternal. Bonnie was ever present with me. Changing my thinking, I began to heal.

I prayed to Bonnie. I started hearing her. Not in the usual way one hears things, but I knew it was her speaking to me. She was coming from my heart. I began to fill my life with all the things that she loved. I thought about everything she loved, what she did that brought her joy, and how she healed herself. I thought, *In pursuing all the things that Bonnie loved, little by little, I can take steps to bring Bonnie back into my life. Then I will find Bonnie.* It worked.

Bonnie brought Mindfulness to me, so I put Mindfulness in my life. I took two mindfulness series and continued my practice daily, which started my journey back to myself. Through meditation, I realized I was not my mother self. I was the observer of the mother self. I began to have compassion for my mother self. I started to send my love for Bonnie to every cell of my body. My body healed. Even years later, I am still on this course. Mindfulness Meditation has been a gift that helps me navigate Grief. I was lucky to be with Bonnie for thirty-six years on earth. It may be the hardest thing I have ever done. The change in our relationship from the physical to the spiritual plane was the answer for me. She is still present with me.

As things proceeded, I found what follows to be true. I am continually having experiences of Bonnie actively involved in my life. I know that Bonnie is part of my spirit team. She is ever-present. Bonnie comes to my assistance eager and willing.

Even with all these new insights, I couldn't ignore Grief, push her away, or block her out by being busy or sick. Eventually, she found her way back in. Grief was persistent. I had to listen to her. She kept telling me I was stuck and had not done all my work. There was more for me. I wasn't going back to the way things used to be. Friendships and interests shifted. She was requiring more from me. There was nothing else I could do. I embraced Grief.

Grief became my friend. First, Grief spent lots of time with me. Over time, we got to know each other well. Then, I invited Grief at a chosen time for a daily hourly visit. I would be with her. Grief liked to play games. She masked as depression or unrest. Eventually, I came to understand her and knew what she wanted. She wanted me to go deeper into my inner world to view something with me. The sooner I did this, the better it was for me.

We looked at "this something" together. It wasn't all work. Sometimes, Grief wanted me to be still. Connect with nature. Be creative. We had fun being together. Over time, my compassion and understanding grew. My appreciation for everything grew. I found joy again. Grief rarely visits anymore, but when she

> *Sometimes, Grief wanted me to be still. Connect with nature. Be creative. We had fun being together. Over time, my compassion and understanding grew. My appreciation for everything grew. I found joy again.*

does, I welcome her. I am present to receive what she brings. Grief makes me a better, wiser, and more loving person. Grief is one of the gateways to the experience of unconditional Divine Love.

The grief process has connected me with something far grander than I could have ever imagined. I have found my inner voice, my inner guidance. I realize that Bonnie is still with me as light. She is now my light daughter. I started to get signs and messages. They brought me comfort and gave me life to continue living. Following my heart, my love for Bonnie led me to joy. I found her in the present moment. And I stay in the present moment.

Being with Bonnie has brought renewed interest in living and appreciating the things of life. Bonnie got me back to Mother Earth. Mother Earth told me, "Now you know how I feel." Those words shot through me! I took her words to heart. Her words motivated me to action. My life transformed. I began to commune with nature and sing. I studied *Ho'oponopono*. I utilized breathing to process what came up in my feeling realm.

My husband and I started the Bonnie Albright Fort Lewis College Teacher Education Scholarship for single mothers. I went to grief counseling and a grief support group. I joined Zumba and Yoga. I studied gardening, became a Colorado Master Gardener, and volunteered in the community gardens and farmer's markets. I made herbal salves, painted, and journaled.

Recently, I received a message from Mother Earth. She told me that I had had enough sorrow. "No more!" She put me on the path to joy. With joy, there is no going into deep sorrow. Now, I notice the sorrow boundary and don't cross it. I listened to Mother Earth. It was evident that it was time for no more sorrow. I am here for joy, to experience the joy in everything, even amidst world chaos.

My highest vision right now: On my path to joy, I accept and love others for who they are as they are. I don't try to change or force anyone. I allow people to be who they are. I allow myself to be who I am. I judge no one. I make choices that bring me joy. I allow groups to

> *I accept and love others for who they are as they are. I don't try to change or force anyone. I allow people to be who they are. I allow myself to be who I am. I judge no one.*

be what they are. Only when I see an opportunity to offer myself for the highest good, do I know why I am present there. I am willing to help. At some point, there is a place for me to offer my gifts. It will drop right in my lap. I don't need to look for it or suggest it. It will happen. I guarantee that.

The power is in my being. My presence alone brings change. Over the years, I've learned that either the person changes or leaves. I don't have to do anything but be myself. Setting aside my agendas, I am away from organizing events, tending to the balance sheets, or running Zoom meetings. Yes, I can do all those things. When I see an opportunity to lift things, I still do. I speak my truth.

I am here to bring the tone, the tone of life, the vibration of the presence of the Divine. The vibration does all the orchestration at an invisible level of creation. Serendipity, synchronicity, puts an appearance in unexpected places, like magic, effortlessly.

Here are the most recent examples of that orchestration from the last twelve months that dropped in my lap: I exhibited my artwork in a three-month exhibit, presented at the worldwide '7 Days of Rest', became board secretary of SW ARC, art chosen for the Red Dress Project fundraiser, invited to write this chapter, and I started my blog.

I have let go of trying to change people or groups. This new internal work is challenging for me. I am always in the change process. I am an agent of change. My past training was: if you see it, it is yours to do; if you see a hole, you fill it. Rather than criticize and complain, you do something to right it. I have the vision. I can see problems. I also see ways for change: it can flow better and be more efficient. I improve it. I make it more focused and more fun. If it's mine, I do it. If someone else wants to do it, I provide support for them. I see it as my responsibility. I am as busy as a beaver. It was who I was for the first sixty-six years of my life. It was a great life. I loved it. I was driven. I never said, "No".

When my daughter Bonnie passed from this earth, I couldn't follow my old ways. They didn't work in the world I was now in. No more pushing, forcing, or making things happen; another way emerged, the way of being. This is revealed as I live love and joy – no more focus on doing.

Now I don't have to do everything. Before, I would see a "problem." Then, I changed my thinking. Now, I see an "opportunity" to send love through the web of light. I trust through loving and giving it up to the Source of Everything to transmute, that the problem will transform. It does. I take care of myself and do what is mine to do. It's a better way for me to live. I see the gifts of life all around me. My world is now lit with love and joy. I prefer the ease of a more natural, balanced life. I no longer carry the weight of the world on my shoulders. Like the eagle with perspective, I see from a place of wisdom.

My path to joy continues.

SPILLING THE TEA ON CHOICE
～ HEIDI CONNOLLY ～

SINCE THE DAY Irene's gracious invitation arrived asking me to contribute to this beautiful book, the idea of choice has never strayed far from my mind. It seems that every day, every choice I've made, from which toothpaste to buy to where I might live, has felt vibrationally intensified, infused with a keener level of awareness. *What is the impact of each choice I make? Do I trust the choices I make? Could the choice of which toothpaste be as important on some level as which place to live?*

In this particular lifetime on the planet as spirit in human form, and in my sixth decade of life, these questions, I have decided, are deserving of my utmost reflection.

The first thing worthy of note is my awareness of how my process around choosing has shifted. Choosing anything, regardless of its size, shape, or potential impact, is no longer laced with that thick edge of panic, the voice insisting that whatever choice I make will surely end in disaster.

For many years, making decisions felt risky and sticky, fraught with the undertones of an emotional maelstrom. Wherever I went, I carried with me the sense that a wrecking ball hovered over my head ready to crush me and my spirit at the slightest perceived misdemeanor. I suppose, without knowing it, I was choosing to believe I had no choice. Still, somehow, even during those panic-laced times and the decisions that arose from them did not hold the same kind of gravitas they do now. Because back then nothing, however painful or scary, seemed irreversible. The scent of renewal, possibility, and option was always out there, somewhere, even if it felt beyond my reach.

Now, irrepressibly, while it's pretty clear there will be fewer choices in my future given the whole less-time-in-front-of-me-than-behind-me thing (at least with linear time as our gauge), I feel freer, wiser, and more empowered to make each choice as it arrives on the doorstep of my soul's gateway.

I guess we all have a tipping point. Mine was the death of my husband in 2012. That's when the universe abjectly refused to sit idly by and let me go down with the ship. I wonder even now, given the arc of my grief, when – if – I ever really consciously made the choice to adjust my course. Exactly when did the blanket of my bereavement lift? I'm still not sure. It's tricky to shift direction when you're barreling headlong down Desperation Road at a hundred miles an hour with the edge of the cliff coming up fast.

Looking back, I realize I must have renewed my soul/human contract over and over, some days more consciously than others, because I stuck around even when the effort of sticking around felt torturously irrelevant. Which is why it's only right to spill the tea here, with all of you. To cop to the fact that it was never me who really made the choice. In fact, it was the choice that made me. One day I woke up and found that life, however inexplicable and unfathomable, had become worth living again.

> *One day I woke up and found that life, however inexplicable and unfathomable, had become worth living again.*

And the tea keeps spilling.

I'm not gonna lie. When my husband began speaking to me from the other side and other spirits jumped on the bandwagon faster than you can say, "Who the heck are you and why are you here?" it was a smack upside the head – only in a good way. I mean, it would be crazy to ignore such a wildly unexpected ability that literally appeared overnight. I kept asking, *Talk to Spirit? Who me? This overly sensitive, underwhelmingly capable, too deeply emotive empath?* Why would *I* be offered the opportunity to chitchat across the veil?

My husband's answer came loud and clear: "Heidi," he said, "I've been trying to talk to you since I kicked the bucket. All you have to do to hear me is stop grieving. If you want a relationship – a new kind of partnership – with me as a Spirit Being, you have to let me go as I was as a physical being."

"Well," I answered, "If you put it like that, I guess I have no choice."

Of course, I did have a choice. But I'd have been nuts to turn down my chance at something I'd wanted for so long, to allow the curtains of my misery to part. At least long enough to let in the crack of light determinedly slogging its way through my resistance.

I can't say it was gung-ho from there, exactly. I proceeded like so many of my clients now who are learning to accept that, while they are absolutely convinced they are the last people on earth capable of hearing from a loved one on the other side, it ain't necessarily so. Just look at the way my own husband had to use the Spirit World's adaptation of a bullhorn in my ear to get me to listen. It was the choice to stop resisting that connection with him, which admittedly came in the form of emphatic, precisely delivered directives (and, yeah, really, really loud!) that changed everything.

Who knew that I'd be in my fifties before I realized that all those indicators from which I suffered (panic attacks, self-doubt, fear, isolation, alienation, anxiety, over-the-top emotional responses, allergies, blah, blah, blah) were all simply forms of resistance to my own potential – in other words, my ability to network with the higher planes of existence. Who knew I'd be in my sixties living the life I'm living by my very own system of Intuitive Logic? It's as if what I call my "Internal Ink," my deep cellular patterns, have been reconfigured into new images that express out in the world the true nature of who I am, along with my purpose on the planet. Who knew I'd have the choice, and choose, to be more than I ever thought I could be?

Who am I now that I wasn't back in my thirties, forties, or fifties? The question keeps popping up like a cork in water that refuses to sink, propelling me into tireless self-reflection. I regard myself in the mirror and wonder where I've gone at the very same time I see exactly who I've become. I see knowledge in eyes that were previously unsure. I see self-love where there was only uncertainty. And I see acceptance of and trust for each decision I make in the here and now.

I can honestly look back in gratitude for the path I've walked and the choices that have mapped out that path — even those constrained by the threatening wrecking ball over my head. More compellingly, I look at each day as an opportunity to discover life in alignment: to make awareness and conscious choice my goal. With my Psychic Octopus tentacles reeled in where they belong (out of other people and the world's energy), I am free to make choices that embrace and reflect both 100% responsibility and 100% freedom. I know with 100% percent conviction that it's how I *feel* as I'm making my choice that is the sole indicator of where I am on the alignment scale when I'm making it.

> I look at each day as an opportunity to discover life in alignment: to make awareness and conscious choice my goal.

One result of this high-frequency selection process that rocks my world is that I have fewer expectations for others to meet my needs. I focus on the choices *I* make, that are *all mine* to make, which frees me up to accept whatever comes next. And that's a heck of a big deal, because in this world where nothing is stagnant, choice remains mandatory.

I can tell you one thing for sure. When I choose from a place of vibrational alignment and loving intention, I no longer have to ques-

> I am appreciating the ease of swimming with the tide, of relaxing into rather than planning for.

tion or worry about potential outcomes, about the what-comes-nexts. I no longer spend my time strategizing Plan A, B, C, and D. Yeah, okay, every once in a while a 3:00 a.m. case of the nerves sneaks up, but I'm only human. The thing that's different is that now, as sure as I am that I can never know what Source will toss my way, I'm just as sure that it has my back, and that flowing with life's situations as they arise is the grooviest way through. I am appreciating the ease of swimming with the tide, of relaxing *into* rather than planning *for*.

Choosing to live from this energetic space makes choice simpler, and therefore easier. It makes navigating life friendlier and vastly more manageable, which manifests a very different kind of reality, one that is wholeheartedly more direct, sound, and satisfying. A reality that I can trust.

Are there times I question how it could possibly have taken me so long to achieve this state of powerfully relaxed awareness? *Um, yeah.* Are there times I wonder at how little I know and how little I feel it is possible to know given the parameters of human consciousness? *Ditto.* On the other hand, I can't tell you how good it feels; the inspirational force behind my actions is a focus on the choice to evolve into ever higher levels of inspired connection. Instead of making the choice to judge where I am, what I know, what I do, and what I have, I choose to make the choice to keep expanding, loving, cherishing, sharing, and appreciating.

My sixties have been filled with more blessings than I could possibly list, including new friendships with brilliant and loving individuals, just like our beloved Irene. People who have made their own choice to share themselves with me with love in their hearts, who have elevated me and helped me choose to elevate myself. Who choose every single day to live in integrity and make choices that benefit themselves *and* others. Blessed and honored to be in their midst, I make the daily choice, validated over and over by how good it feels, to stand by their side.

Do I still agonize about what to wear? Well, duh . . . like I said, I'm only human. But from there it's a quick recalibration and I'm reminded that it's not the logical choice, but the internal, intuitively guided one, that brings on all the happy feels.

Choosing by default is going through life on autopilot, choices about toothpaste or which Netflix to binge-watch notwithstanding. Conscious choice is not about making that list of pros and cons, as society so stridently advises, and applying "logical" suppositions, standards, measurements, and facts. Instead, it's about using your Intuitive Guidance System (IGS), the one that gets switched on as soon as you're in alignment and moves you from where you are to the next step, to the next, and on to the next. Sure, it may feel that you never quite arrive since you're only focused on choosing that next step, but that's what makes life – yup, you heard it here – all about putting the journey ahead of the destination.

And *that's* the choice that's truly good to the last drop.

HOW I MET MYSELF
MARY D'AGOSTINO

I NEVER EXPECTED TO enter the third chapter of life grieving the loss of my youngest son. The first two chapters rarely offered up the expected. I entered young adulthood and unexpectedly became a mother at the tender age of eighteen. Then again at twenty. I married and divorced and faced single motherhood by age twenty-two. I married again a few years later and had three more children. Expectations moved aside to make room for the unexpected. Abandonment, mental illness, addiction, domestic violence, economic hardship, and raising a child with congenital heart disease were some of the unexpected experiences I lived with, and through. And with each unexpected challenge, I dug deep and made choices that led me to meet my truest self.

Motherhood came naturally as the eldest of eight siblings. I mothered someone ever since I can remember. My own mother included. Mothering is a touchstone, an identity I am familiar with, bringing fulfillment and pushing me to grow in ways that nothing else could. I devoted my life to raising my children. Each one, beautiful and unique. I was their greatest advocate, nurturing a strong sense of self-esteem and unconditional love. I tried my best to provide them with what I wished I had growing up.

I was relentlessly challenged. Not in my devotion or dedication, but with how much support I would or would not have. I learned that those I expected would be my allies were not. Family, friends, the fathers of my children, society, and religion, all posed various threats to my desire to instill a healthy sense of self-identity, esteem, and belonging for my children and myself.

I learned how to love and support myself through the unexpected turmoil and betrayals. My children's fathers each brought their own brand of pain into the marriages and into how they parented. Through it all I kept reaching deep, meeting myself in the pain and joys and persevered for them.

> The more I became myself, the more a true sense of soul esteem emerged.

I also wanted to live a full life and sought to pursue formal education, my passions being in writing and art, creative expression, personal growth, and complementary healing modalities. My personal pursuits were often met with resistance, shame, and guilt by others. I pursued them anyway. I was meeting myself and discovered great joy in learning and expanding my awareness beyond that which others told me I could be or do. Slowly, I freed myself of others and my own ideas, of what was expected of me and who I was supposed to be. The more I became myself, the more a true sense of soul esteem emerged. Divorcing the second husband when I was well into my second chapter allowed for a new surge of creative energy to be released, and I built a healthy and loving environment for me and my children. Encouragement, compassion, patience, and support were staples. Hard truths could be faced with loving kindness rather than denied. Challenges were ongoing, yet I could meet them in my wholeness instead of brokenness. I met myself and discovered my way forward.

Perhaps this is how I gathered the courage to face the greatest challenge of my life: the death of my youngest son. He was a mere twenty-four years of age when he was killed instantly in a single car collision in early 2017. Unexpected, sudden, and tragic. He was a true light. A kind young man with a heart of gold. How could I meet myself in this?

I would need the greatest medicines of all to put my shattered heart back together. Medicine for the body, mind, and soul. I promised myself and my children that we would figure out how to grieve and live on after the unspeakable loss. A promise not unlike the one I made for myself when I unexpectedly became a mother at the age of eighteen. I did not know how, but I would meet myself in unspeakable loss.

I met myself first with a daily question: What do I need today? I was trained to first ask others what do *you* need? Tending to others does give me satisfaction, yet I couldn't lift a finger to tend, if I tried. Most days, I met myself with simple needs: rest, food, sunshine. That was enough.

I met myself by creating and maintaining my home as a nest; a nurturing, healing environment that sat high in a fir tree, figuratively. I wrapped my body in warm, soft blankets, inviting in angels to comfort me. My home *had a heart and a soul* and became a safe place where no one and nothing could interfere with my healing process. I met myself, to paraphrase Mark Twain "... *in its grace, and in the peace of its benediction ... [I] could not enter it unmoved.*" I met myself with compassion. A true elixir that eases the pain of life's greatest challenges. Compassion is an art to be practiced, a muscle to build. Fierce compassion guided me to care for myself slowly, and with the truth that you can never rush the healing.

I met myself with kindness. Kindness offers a buffering place within, where I retreat when the harshness of the world gets too close. The walls of my nest are layered with kindness.

I met myself with nonjudgment, continuously releasing the heavy stones of judgment and criticism that weigh heavy on a grieving mother's heart. Nonjudgment releases the unforgiving need to criticize, critique or shame my progress and feelings. It allows the construction within the destruction of loss.

I met myself in the knowing that no two people grieve alike. How I met myself may not be helpful to another. Applying compassion, kindness, and nonjudgment helps, no matter where or how a fellow human needs to be met.

I met myself with open-minded trust in what my body needed. I stopped pushing my body to be something it is not. When I am tired, I rest. When I can't sleep, I use soothing music and meditation apps. So many good ones, so easily accessed. I met myself with a deep understanding about grief as a physiological process that is overpowering and exhausting. I met myself with salt baths and massages, cranial sacral work, and body gentleness. I met myself with healers who could meet me with trauma awareness.

I met myself by feeling. Feeling is healing and the feelings that surface when walking the path of grief are immense, and unbearable at times. I met myself by going through these feelings of rage, anger, and searing pain with great care and patience. I met myself on the other side. With grace.

I met myself human to spirit. I accept my humanness, and my emotional, mental, and physical needs. I accept my Spirit self and let her guide me in sweet connections with my son in spirit, the magical synchronicities, signs, and symbols that give me exactly what I need to trust in the places of spirit, higher consciousness, and dimensions beyond the earth bond. I found great solace in the places where my human self in all its suffering met my Spirit self in healing eternal love.

> *Feeling is healing and the feelings that surface when walking the path of grief are immense, and unbearable at times.*

I met myself in deep knowing and faith. Not in a religious concept, but in love I shared with my son and will continue to share. I met myself in a continued relationship with him. I am still his mother. Here I found miracles beyond explanation. Miracles continue to remind me, there is more to life than meets the human eye alone.

I met myself through the hearts and sweet faces of my grown children and grandchildren. I met myself in their hugs and smiles, meals shared, tears shed, silliness and joy. I met myself in their milestones and everyday life, hardships, and triumphs. I met myself with them.

I met myself each morning as I greeted the day, unsure if I could. I met myself in whatever frame of mind I found myself. This was the hardest part, to meet myself in sadness or terror and try not to move it too soon. I met myself in the moment when it was all I had room for in the confines of a mind trying to make sense of the nonsensical.

I met myself at the end of the day. With gratitude. I counted the days. I still do. I met myself in making each day matter. I met myself in reverence for the moments, and the hours and with the revelation of hidden knowledge that so many deny. Life is short. No one knows how many days we have. Let's make the most of each day and look for the love. Sometimes hidden, sometimes out in the open, yet always there.

I met myself by honoring my deep inner knowing of ritual and ceremony. Ancestors, mothers in my lineage who also lost children came to me in dreams offering their wisdom and love. Did they meet themselves? I would do it for them and for my children's children. I lit the candles and fires, sat with trees, made prayer mandalas and bundles filled tight. I met myself as I applied rituals that are containers of pure love and self-respect. I lifted many a prayer up and into the winds of healing. I met myself as an Ancestor, Ancient, Healer, and Priestess.

I met myself walking in nature, having playlists titled "Walking in Healing Love". I read little and when I did it was always inspirational words that would stick. All the rest fell out, like leaves on a cold autumn day or warm tears running down my face.

I met myself by validating what I endured, acknowledging my courageous and brave heart. I met myself as my fierce protector. I met myself with hope, encouragement, overflowing love and promise that healing can and does occur. Everything superfluous fell away. Everything timeless stayed. The noise of outer opinions mattered not.

I met myself with grief counseling, art therapy, and grief group support. Grief is not an illness. It is a time and place that honors how much I love. I did not push myself, nor admonish myself if I was not up for it. I allowed gentle feelings to mix with the deep burdensome sadness. What I created in art gave my body space to hold the soupy mixture or became a place to hold it outside of myself and gaze at the immense beauty of grief given form.

I met myself with forgiveness and a deep knowing that sprung like confidence up from the ashes of the past. I provided my son with much love, guidance and unwavering support and this truth did emerge to meet me. I could have done more, yet this was not a place I ever stayed in. It held no healing, just shame.

> I made peace with the truth that our minds can break in times of deep grief.

I met myself with forgiveness for others when they could not or would not meet me. I met myself when acts unforgiveable were thrust upon me in the throes of my loss by people and family who professed to love me. I met forgiveness as a journey, that I do not fully understand. I learned its balm is a surrender of sorts. A willingness to let go of the unforgiving actions of others and continue to meet myself with peace of mind.

I met myself by not having to have answers to the unanswerable. The mind will ceaselessly try to find answers to the unanswerable questions of death, trauma, and tragedy. If only and why became sharp daggers inserted into open wounds. I made peace with the truth that our minds can break in times of deep grief. I met myself in my broken mind, calling in peace as the needle and thread, glue, and gold that would weave my broken mind and heart back together. Grieving is weaving.

I met myself setting boundaries on my time and energy by not explaining or proving my needs, decisions, or actions. I met myself on shaky ground. I said no. I said yes. I changed my mind on shaky ground. I met myself by commanding my boundaries and knowing this was the territory of no compromise. I met myself in growing trust that shaky ground would indeed hold me and my wizened, battle-weary heart.

I met myself in friendships with loving and kind people, soul kin. Very few and select. Some long-time friends, others new, many who were learning to meet themselves through life's deepest challenges too. I savored the moments in silence with my people. We openly wept and held one another, blessing each other with our tears. We know the otherworldly joys and sorrows and in the depths of this real human connection, we heal, thrive, and find ways to laugh again.

I met myself in the mending and weaving of safety nets through the most hazardous of life experiences. I met myself in being a dispenser and receiver of the exact right medicine at the exact right time. A knowing of the miracles of interconnectedness, of life after death, and how spirit works to ensure our safe passage through the most trying of times. I met myself by being an answer to a prayer and by being in service to love.

I met myself with writing poetry, journaling, teaching, sacred circle gatherer. I met myself in my shattered heart as self-healer, medicine woman, wise elder, broken mother, and devastated child. I met myself in all the shattered pieces and in the depths of my soul.

Through it all, I became the woman I was always meant to be. I am both a work in progress and a masterpiece. This is me in the third chapter of life, living each day as an opportunity to meet myself and others in safe and sacred spaces, offering a compassionate healing practice for those hungering to meet themselves and nourish their soul.

My days are devoted to a solidification of my service to self, family, community, and humanity to continue to heal and grow through shared stories, sacred healing practices, creative expression, and the sharing of my deep knowing that come from places discovered as I met myself. One sacred step at a time. My profession as Astrologer, Healer, Intuitive, Author and Teacher are where I meet myself and you.

I won't retire, for that would be silly. Life is just beginning. Again.

CONTRIBUTORS

Anita Albright, BA, MA is a wife, mother, and grandmother on a lifelong journey of integrity and personal growth. With over thirty-two years of experience in teaching, Anita has educated students from various backgrounds and abilities, including those with dyslexia, autism spectrum disorders, and emotional and behavioral challenges. She firmly believes in teaching through experiential learning, making education a fun and engaging experience. Anita holds a BA in Psychology and Elementary Education, as well as an MA in Special Education: Mild to Moderate Needs. She has also received extensive training in teaching methods such as Orton Gillingham, Lindamood Bell, Wilson Reading, and Visualizing Verbalizing. In retirement, Anita continues to contribute to her community. She serves on the board of SW Colorado ARC. She also practices mindful meditation, Reiki, and Sound Healing. Anita's hobbies include writing, art, gardening, and time spent in nature.

You can contact Anita at
thankfulgrandma.blog or anitaalbright8@gmail.com

Angela Clement is a former school principal and currently a speaker, writer, energy healer and the creator and host of the *Awaken Your Soul's Journey* series on grief. When her husband Blaine was diagnosed with stage four colon cancer in January 2021, Angela used her knowledge of energy healing to help him with his symptoms and her through the intense emotion. After he transitioned in October 2021, she continued her study, seeking support from healers and coaches to help her. She has since hosted four online summits interviewing over one hundred experts in grief. This information has helped her expand her new life and build a supportive community. Angela is passionate about helping others who are grieving to find hope and live a life of joy and meaning after loss. As a certified grief coach, Angela provides one-on-one and group grief support and healing for those suffering from loss. For more information, please visit https://healingenergy.world/.

Heidi Connolly is an author, book shepherd, intuitive medium, life coach, and musician whose books include *Crossing the Rubicon* (a journey through grief), *The Gateway Café* (a metaphysical novel of interdimensional travel) and *Elevating Your HSP-ness* (for "HyPerceptive" individuals everywhere!). Heidi's mediumship skill connects clients with their loved ones on the other side to receive messages of love and guidance; her work with Highly Sensitive People (HyPerceptives) focuses on helping them develop their own brilliant gifts. A spirit-guided musician, Heidi's flute recordings are renowned for the healing power of their encoded frequencies. Her new 8-module video course, *The HSP Treatment Breakthrough*, guides participants through unique, powerful developmental tools and techniques (including the Psychic Octopus, Internal Inking, and the Unique Energetic Signature), while her newest book, *Playing With Your Higher Self: Psychic Games for Your Intuitive Muscle*, offers the most engaging way *ever* to dip your intuitive toe into the water – or thrash about in the deep end. For further information, please visit www.Heidiconnolly.com.

Mary D'Agostino, CRMT/P is a mother, teacher, artist, author, healer, and owner of Heart of Gaia Creative Healing Arts. She weaves together the Intuitive Arts of Astrology, Mediumship, Energy Medicine, Spiritual Counsel, and Journaling as offerings to clients and students who seek to awaken their inherent wisdom, healing, and insight. As storyteller, she helps awaken the hidden truths of our most true nature. Her first novel *Into the Forest, A Maiden's Journey,* was published in 2020 and the second in this series is due out in December 2024. For grief support, her book *111 Days of Divine Inspiration* is a companion daybook to guide us through the most challenging days of bereavement with hope in the miracles of life. Mary is here to offer her continued healing guidance and compassionate support for a most inspiring life journey through all of life's chapters. For further information, please visit www.marydagostino.com.

Casey Gauntt, B.S., JD, MBA, is a retired attorney and former senior executive of a major San Diego real estate company. In 2011, Casey launched his website Write Me Something Beautiful: A journey of loss, love and discovery to share the healing journey he embarked on following the accidental death of his son Jimmy and the suicide of his father three decades earlier. In 2013, Casey co-founded a group of fathers in San Diego who have lost children. They call themselves the "Fraternity," have grown to over twenty-five brothers, and meet regularly. Casey lives in Solana Beach, California with his wife of over fifty years, Hilary. Their daughter, Brittany, son-in-law, Ryan, and three grandchildren live close by.

Yvonne Heath, RN worked in the United States and Canada as a registered nurse for twenty-seven years in emergency, chemotherapy, palliative care, and hospice. She became disheartened by society's reluctance to prepare for grief, transitions, and death – causing excessive suffering. She suffered too, not knowing how to do it differently. In 2015 she blazed a new trail to create social change and founded *Love Your Life to Death* and the *I Just Showed Up Movement.* She shares her message with heart and humor as an author, speaker and trainer. Her *TEDx Talk:* Transforming our Grief, by *Just Showing Up* has been viewed by thousands. As empty nesters, Yvonne and husband Geordie can be found wearing socks and sandals in their happy place in Muskoka, Canada. For further information, please visit www.loveyourlifetodeath.com.

Tami Hendrix is an intuitive animal communicator, compassionate medium, and healer committed to helping relationships transform on every level. Her childhood experiences helped her forge a deep, compassionate connection with all beings, allowing her to see the true essence of any soul or situation. As a result, she has a soul-level awareness to communicate with animals emotionally, mentally, and spiritually. Since she maintains a private animal sanctuary, she has first-hand experience with many different animals and situations. Her style is conversational and natural and leaves no doubt you are connecting with your pet. Additionally, her work with James Van Praagh in mediumship development classes has solidified her passion to help pets who have crossed over connect with their humans in a beautiful way, resulting in healing from grief and broken hearts and finding a renewed sense of purpose. For further information, please visit Soul-Speak with Tami Hendrix at https://tamihendrix.com/.

Mark Ireland is the cofounder of Helping Parents Heal, an organization with more than 26,000 members that assists bereaved parents worldwide. He has participated in mediumship research studies conducted by the University of Arizona and the University of Virginia, and currently operates a Medium Certification program. The author of *Soul Shift*, and *The Persistence of the Soul*, he lives in Camas, Washington. For further information, please visit: www.markirelandauthor.com/.

Betty Jampel, MSW, LCSW has over thirty years of experience as a clinical social worker and holistic psychotherapist. She practices from a transpersonal and humanistic framework that centers around cultivating psychospiritual growth. Betty does not shy away from working with non-ordinary states of consciousness and is trained to provide Ketamine-Assisted Psychotherapy (KAP) as well as Psychedelic Medicine Integration as part of a treatment plan. Betty strives to create a safe and compassionate space for individuals navigating the complexities of life, death, and loss. Guided by love, compassion, and understanding of the whole individual within a complex system, she aims to foster understanding, healing, and resolution at the intersection of life's most poignant moments. For further information, please visit: www.psychologytoday.com/us/therapists/betty-jampel-springfield-nj/757324.

Frances Rae Key is a writer of songs, scripts, and books that seek to express a perspective from the "lookout tower of the soul." Many of her songs of peace and goodwill have been performed by choirs around the world, and her musical *Aussie Song* won Best Music in the NYC Theatrefest in 2019. After the passing of her mother in 2010, Frances had a profound experience of communication with her from the Other Side, resulting in four volumes of spiritual insights titled *The Team: A Mother's Wisdom from the Other Side.* Since then, she has shared her life-changing experience widely through public presentations and has written a novel, *The Train to Hoffehausen,* and a screenplay based upon it, which expresses in fictionalized form the spiritual principles described in the books. Frances is the mother of four and grandmother of twelve, a treasure she values most deeply. You can learn more about Frances's many projects at www.FrancesKey.net.

Shirley Lister – In 2016, Shirley's youngest son Cam, received a life-changing diagnosis. It was the catalyst for her to learn all she could and when he succumbed to the disease, to share it to stop others from experiencing this needless tragedy. Alongside this, she immediately began to get signs from her son that she couldn't ignore as anything other than communication from him. As a result, she is the author of *Soul Signs: A Recipe for Miracles*, a workbook guide for those grieving to catalogue the signs they have been receiving. There are no coincidences! Recently, Shirley retired from her nearly 30-year career as an Education Assistant and moved to the East Coast of Canada with her husband of thirty-two years and little dog, Juno. They have one other son who lives in one of the Prairie Provinces.

Mary Metcalfe, BJ, MS has over forty-five years of experience in consulting, researching, writing, and editing on a wide range of health and well-being subjects including child well-being, active living and older adults, violence against women, reproductive technologies, disabilities, patient privacy issues, etc. Her projects have resulted in numerous government reports, newspaper, and journal articles as well as online resources. She is a former partner of a management consulting firm and founded three successful private companies. In 2005, she founded Not Just Tourists – Ottawa, whose volunteers collect and distribute donated medical supplies to local groups and over ninety countries in need around the world. Mary lives on a small lake in rural Quebec with her husband of forty-six years, their dog and cat, and assorted wildlife large and small.

Phyllis Okon is a gifted medium who saw her life take a new direction when her husband of over forty years transitioned. Her background as a teacher, CEO, best-selling and award-winning author, as well as wife, mother, and grandmother, all contributed to her becoming established as a compassionate and understanding medium. She also studied with several well-known names in mediumship. So, when her husband passed, she learned that their relationship hadn't ended but had moved to a new plane. To this day, her husband has remained in her life to become her guide in helping others connect with their loved ones. For further information, please visit: https://ladyphyllis.com/.

Ellie Pechet, M.Ed. is a Meta-physician, Medium, Shaman, and author with over thirty-three years in the intuitive counseling/energy healing field. Clients worldwide benefit by her remote healing from the comfort of their own home via Skype, Google Meet phone, and in person in her Orange County, CA office. Ellie's high success rate (over 93%) in permanently eliminating clients' emotional and physical issues and conditions sets her apart from other healers, practitioners, and therapists. She offers Medical Intuitive Scans to find root causes of symptoms and identify energy blocks. Ellie heals Grief, Depression, PTSD, Anxiety, Physical and Emotional Abuse, specific Traumas, Insomnia, and viruses such as COVID-19, Lyme, HPV, Chronic Pain, Fibromyalgia, and other conditions. Ellie also dialogues with deceased Spirits as described in her book *Hitching A Ride: A Guide to Earthbound Spirits and How They Affect You*. For further information, please visit www.phoenixrisinghealing.com.

Mark Pitstick, MA, DC, has over fifty years of experience helping many people in hospitals, pastoral counseling settings, mental health centers and holistic health care clinics. After working with dying persons, including children, he was motivated to find evidence-based answers to life's biggest questions including: 'Who am I? Why am I here? Is there really life after bodily death?' Mark's book *The Afterlife Evidence* shares scientific, clinical, and experiential evidence to the last question. He directs the SoulPhone Foundation, assists research on the SoulPhone Project, and works closely with the HelpingParentsHeal.org organization. Dr. Pitstick also presents frequent webinars for IANDS.org and HumanitysTeam.org. To learn more, visit SoulProof.com and SoulPhone.com.

Jeff Rasley, BA, JD, MDiv is a lawyer and has taught classes on philanthropy and community development at Butler and Marian Universities. He is the author of fourteen books and over ninety articles in academic journals and mainstream periodicals, including *Newsweek, Chicago Magazine, ABA Journal*, and *Family Law Review*. He is an award-winning photographer. His pictures taken in the Himalayas, Caribbean, and Pacific islands have been published in several journals. He has been a featured guest on over 150 radio and podcast programs. Jeff is founder and president of the Basa Village Foundation, which raises money for culturally sensitive development in the Basa area of Nepal. He is president of the Scientech Foundation of Indiana, which issues grants of $250,000 per year to STEAM programs in Indiana. He is also the US liaison for Nepal-based Adventure Geo-Treks; a partner in Midsummer Books; a director of the Indianapolis

Peace and Justice Center; and, co-founder of the Jeff & Alicia Rasley Internship Program for ACLU of Indiana. For further information, please visit http://jeffreyrasley.com/.

Julie Lazar-Reskakis, BS, MS is currently employed at Holy Name Medical Center in Teaneck, NJ. She is a Certified Grief Educator, Perinatal Bereavement Specialist, End of Life Doula and Birth Doula. She is passionate about helping families through pregnancy and infant loss. She can be reached at: JALR124@aol.com. In her spare time, Julie enjoys cake decorating, reading, hiking, and spending time with her friends and family.

Faust Ruggiero, MS has pursued his professional career for over forty years. He has counseled individuals and families in inpatient facilities, prisons, substance abuse counseling centers, in nursing homes; provided employee assistance programs to major corporations; and has extensive experience providing emotional support services to deaf children, veterans, first responders, law enforcement, and other emergency personnel. He developed the 'Process Way of Life' and has used it with over two thousand clients, helping them to realize and unleash the power they have inside themselves. With the Process Way of Life being so successful as a counseling program, he has authored the Award-winning Fix Yourself Empowerment Series. Three books have been published: *The Fix Yourself Handbook*, *The Fix Your Anxiety Handbook*, and *The Fix Your Depression Handbook*. *The Fix Your Anger Handbook* is currently being written. For further information, please visit www.faustruggiero.com.

Julie Ryan, BA is a Psychic Medium and Medical Intuitive who can sense what medical conditions and illnesses a person has and facilitate energetic healings. She can communicate with spirits both alive and dead. Julie can scan animals, access people's past lives, and can tell how close to death someone is. Her book *Angelic Attendants: What Really Happens As We Transition From This Life Into The Next* describes a series of events that involves angels, multitudes of deceased family and friends, the spirits of deceased pets, and countless serendipitous and miraculous moments. Julie's Angel Messages® books are picture books that have angels answering kids' tough questions. Each week, Julie scans callers on her *Ask Julie Ryan* show, which is heard by millions in over one hundred countries throughout the world. Julie's Psychic and Medical Intuitive skills are learned. For further information, please visit https://askjulieryan.com.

Brian Smith, BSChE is a Grief Guide and Mental Fitness Trainer. His mission is to help people rediscover who they are and why they are here. Brian believes that the key to thriving in life is understanding who we are, where we came from, and where we are going. Brian began this work shortly after the untimely passing of his 15-year-old daughter Shayna in the summer of 2015. Brian had overcome an extreme fear of death before Shayna's passing. He now believes that he and Shayna are on a mission to help others heal, overcome fear, and regain purpose and passion. Brian hosts the Grief 2 Growth podcast and is the author of *Grief 2 Growth – Planted, Not Buried*.

Alan Stein, BBA, MBA was a City Commissioner in Parkland, a Florida Life/Health and Property/Casualty Insurance Agent, with non-resident licenses in over forty states; a Certified Insurance Counselor (CIC); and, founder of a non-profit organization in Parkland. He also founded multiple companies: Nationwide Club Administrators, Insurance Strategies, ASI Agency, and Strategic Marketing Associates, Inc., to sell credit and warranty-related insurance products. While president and owner of these companies, he developed new products, identified new markets, and subsequently managed corresponding nationwide sales. During his insurance career, Alan worked as an employee and then as an agent for American Bankers Insurance Group, and as an agent for both Central National Insurance Group and Voyager Insurance Company, which were all eventually acquired by Assurant Insurance Company. As of January 2024, Alan is president of First Boca Associates, Inc, a mergers and acquisitions firm, and president of Sell Smart Strategies, Inc., a management consulting firm for online performance management on website platforms like Amazon, Walmart, Shopify, etc.

Mergers and Acquisitions: www.firstboca.net

Amazon: www.sellsmartstrategies.com

Roz Weinberger, BA is a mother, grandmother, artist, community activist, and hard-working person who has pursued multiple 'mini' careers over some fifty years. In her early careers, she was an immigration specialist for the government of Israel and later an American tech firm; manager of a martial arts studio, corporate manager in a 32-store national furniture chain, and self-employed artist in ceramic pottery. She became a licensed Personal Trainer in her sixties, which she continues to this day while also serving as an Assistant Property Manager for Taylor Management in New Jersey.

Bob Wells received his elementary education in a railway school car and homeschooling in Northwestern Ontario, Canada and later graduated high school in the state of Wisconsin. He turned down a free university education and instead chose a life of being a fishing/hunting guide, fur trapper, and a thirty-year career as an Ontario Conservation Officer. Bob is the author of two non-fiction histories: *Mile Post 104 and Beyond* and *Wawahte*, the histories of three Indian Residential School survivors. In 2017, Bob was awarded Canada's highest civilian award – the Sovereign's Medal for Volunteers – for his lifelong contributions to the betterment of Canadian society. Bob lives in a Stittsville, Ontario retirement residence near his son Perry, daughter-in-law Rachel, and grandson Jordan and his partner Liza.

ACKNOWLEDGMENTS

GOOD TO THE LAST DROP! wouldn't have been possible without the collaboration of many. The idea for the book initially came from my great love and beloved husband, Saul, my mom, and others on the Other Side. I feel their love, guidance, and support daily as I continue to live my best life in my third chapter and encourage others around the world to do the same through my podcasts, website, videos, books, and personal contacts and support.

Supporting me in this ongoing journey is my incredibly wonderful and competent assistant Jaidine Stoutt-Williams. Her friendship and professionalism mean the world to me as we continue to navigate the podcast and social media landscape from our respective bases in New Jersey and Barletta, Italy.

I am also forever grateful to Tom Hazzard and his Podetize team that so beautifully produces my popular and inspiring podcasts, which are watched around the world and regularly downloaded. Tom and his team, along with my remarkable Social Media Team, Masters In Clarity, have brought the healing messages from my Grief and Rebirth podcast to hundreds of thousands of people who have experienced profound loss and helped them find their way back to joy and renewed purpose.

There are so many others who have helped and supported me on my journey to healing myself and others:

- Those who have helped me to heal my personal trauma and better understand/process my life and my choices so that I can have this very fulfilling third chapter;
- The loving support of my family and friends;
- The many healers, mediums, therapists, and coaches I have worked with and/or interviewed over the years;
- All the wonderful contributors to this book, who freely volunteered their support and wrote their chapters to encourage all readers to embrace 'possibilities' for a positive future and renewed joy in living;
- My Canadian editor Mary Metcalfe, who helped me develop and craft a vision for this book that will encourage all readers to see their way forward.

Many more people have supported my efforts to make a difference. They are too numerous to list here. Please know that I cherish that support and feel blessed in every way.

LOOKING FOR IRENE?

1. To learn more about Irene and her rebirth journey visit her website: ireneweinberg.com
2. Listen to Grief and Rebirth on Spotify and Apple Podcasts
3. Speak Up Talk Radio's International Positive Change Podcast Award Winner: https://www.speakuptalkradio.com/podcast-award-winners/
4. Subscribe to the Grief and Rebirth YouTube channel to never miss an episode: https://www.youtube.com/@IreneWeinberg
5. Visit the Grief and Rebirth Bookshop to browse books by our inspiring guests: https://bookshop.org/shop/griefandrebirth
6. Sign up for the Grief and Rebirth newsletter to stay up-to-date on forthcoming episodes, events, healing tools, and announcements: https://ireneweinberg.com/#signup
7. Connect with Irene on Facebook, Instagram, and TikTok @irenesweinberg
8. Hear what our incredible guests and listeners of Grief and Rebirth: Finding the Joy in Life Podcast say about their experience: https://ireneweinberg.com/podcast-testimonials/
9. Access The Live Your Most Evolved Life Summit replay: https://ireneweinberg.thinkific.com/courses/all-access-pass-summit-replay-2023
10. Helping Parents Heal Series: https://ireneweinberg.com/helping-parents-heal-2022/

THEY SERVE BAGELS IN HEAVEN

Kindle

Paperback

Audio

GRIEF AND REBIRTH PODCAST

Apple Podcasts

Spotify Podcast

SUGGESTIONS FOR ONLINE REFERENCES[4]

Subject	Website	URL
Grief and Loss	Baby Loss Family Advisors: Helping families when a baby dies	www.babylossfamilyadvisors.org
	Blessing the Bridge: What Animals Teach Us About Death, Dying and Beyond	https://blessingthebridge.com/home
	Canadian Virtual Hospice	www.virtualhospice.ca
	Center for Loss	www.Centerforloss.com
	Early Pregnancy Loss Association Podcast: Hope Blooms	https://www.miscarriagecare.com/ https://hopeblooms.buzzsprout.com/
	Grief 2 Growth: Planted Not Buried	www.grief2growth.com/navigating-spiritual-wisdom-from-beyond-the-veil/
	Waiting Room Revolution: 7 Keys to Feeling Hopeful and Prepared When Dealing with Serious Illness (Podcast)	www.waitingroomrevolution.com

---

4 The above information resources were recommended by the various chapter contributors. Their inclusion here is not an explicit endorsement. Each link was confirmed to be accurate and current at time of publication.

Living Your Best Life	Eden Energy Medicine and Energy Psychology	https://edenenergymedicine.com/
	Green Hope Farm – Flower Essences Animal Wellness issues and essences	https://www.greenhopeessences.com/
	Love Your Life to Death	liveyourlifetodeath.com
	Sonia Choquette: Divine Guides	https://soniachoquette.net/
	Still Sexy After Sixty: Seven Secrets to Finding Life's Sweet Spot	StillSexyAfterSixty.com

SELECTED BIBLIOGRAPHY

Connolly, Heidi and Helen Lang. *Playing With Your Higher Self: Psychic Games for Your Intuitive Muscle* (2Lakes Publishing, 2024).

D'Agostino, Mary. *111 Days of Divine Inspiration* (Renosf.org, 2023). Downloadable as PDF or Epub at https://renosf.org/book/111days-of-divine-intervention.

Gauntt, Casey and Jimmy Gauntt. *Suffering Is the Only Honest Work* (CreateSpace, 2015).

—— *When the Veil Comes Down* (Kindle, 2021).

Kessler, David. *Finding Meaning: The Sixth Stage of Grief.* (New York: Scribner, 2020).

Key, Gloria "Teddy" and Frances Key. *The Team: A Mother's Wisdom from the Other Side, Book 1, 2, 3* and *Beyond the Team: A Mother's Wisdom from the Other Side*, 4-book series (CreateSpace, 2011–2017).

Rasley, Jeff. *72 Wisdoms: A practical guide to make life more meaningful* (Kindle, Audiobook, 2022).

Ireland, Mark. *Soul Shift: Finding Where the Dead Go* (Frog Books, 2008).

——*The Persistence of the Soul: Mediums, Spirit Visitations, and Afterlife Communication* (Inner Traditions, 2023).

Lyster, Shirley. *Soul Signs: A Recipe for Miracles* (Kindle, 2022).

Pechet, Ellie. *Hitching A Ride: A Guide to Earthbound Spirits and How They Affect You* (CreateSpace, 2015).

Pitstick, Mark. *The Afterlife Evidence: Comforting and Convincing Proof that No One Really Dies.* (Waterside Productions, 2022).

Ruggierro, Faust. *The Fix Yourself Handbook; The Fix Your Anxiety Handbook; The Fix Your Depression Handbook;* and *The Fix Your Anger Handbook* (FYHB Publishing, 2019–2024).

Ryan, Julie. *Angelic Attendants: What Really Happens As We Transition From This Life Into The Next.* (Clement, 2017). Audio and Digital copy available for free download at http://julieryangift.com.

Smith, Brian D. *Grief 2 Growth – Planted, Not Buried.* (Brian D. Smith, www.amazon.com/Grief-Growth-Planted-Greatest-Challenges/dp/1079128719.

COMING FALL 2024

THE 2ND EDITION OF *THEY SERVE BAGELS IN HEAVEN* WITH NEW AND EXPANDED MATERIAL NOT PUBLISHED PREVIOUSLY.

TURN THE PAGE TO READ AN EXCERPT!

EXCERPT
THEY SERVE BAGELS IN HEAVEN

"

I THINK MY SOUL left even before my body died. The pain of living, especially over the last eight years, had become such a burden that this sudden moment filled me with profound relief. My last earthly recollection is driving, and then . . . this immense loosening and lightening. For an instant, anyway. Then Irene called out my name, pulling me far enough back into my body so I could handle this accident in a way that made sure she lived through it. That was my final gut instinct: to steer the car so the accident would be the least destructive to her and to make sure that no one else would be harmed. I also knew in every fiber of my being this absolutely would be the last time I would hear her call my name.

After the accident, I left my body and was outside the car. From where I stood, I could see my body slumped over the steering wheel. Even though I knew something awful had happened to me, all I could focus on was Irene. Was she all right? Was she going to live? As I looked around for help, I began to realize that while I was seeing, hearing, and thinking, I had no body. But there wasn't time to process this wacky thought because Irene was in mortal danger. If I had any faculties left at all, I was going to use them to help her.

Despite my concern, it dawned on me that my wife, the car, and the bare winter trees weren't all I could see. Surrounding Irene was a brilliant emerald and blue light that extended to the growing number of people who had stopped to help. It permeated each and every one of them with a magnificent purple light. More than the beauty and wonder of this light was that it held within it angels – honest-to-God angels. In that instant, I understood they were there to protect us – all of us – before they helped me cross over.

My knowing somehow came through the intensity of the radiance in which they held me. The warmth and strength of that radiance reassured me, helping me accept the fact that my life force, my bodiless soul, was now safely cocooned in love and light.

Made in the USA
Columbia, SC
21 June 2024